BORN TO PREACH:

My Testimony & The Revelation

DON LOFTIS

BookTrail Agency
8838 Sleepy Hollow Rd.
Kansas City, MO 64114

Printed in the United States of America

Osie John Henry and Sally Will lived in a small town in Alabama during the years of Jim Crow and segregation in the South. Osie John Henry was a descendant of Europeans and Africans. His grandfather was a white plantation owner who married one of the slave women. In the segregated South, this was not supposed to happen because it was legally unlawful to intermarry, but this is a true story. Sally Will grew up in Mississippi in a small town called Caldonia which was very close to the Alabama border. Fayette, where Osie John Henry grew up was near the Mississippi border. Fayette was in a dry county in Alabama. Mississippi was a wet state where alcoholic beverages were sold freely. On the weekends, Osie John Henry and his friends would travel to Mississippi to drink and have what they called fun, whisky and women at the colored beer Joints in Mississippi.

Osie was primarily a farmer, but each year after the crops had been laid-by, he would get a job with the railroad or some construction company. While in Mississippi on a construction job Osie met Sally one night at a dance. Osie introduced himself and they exchanged addresses so they could stay connected. Osie could not get Sally out of his mind. He had never seen a woman as beautiful as Sally. It was love at first sight. Sally was reared by her grandmother. Her mother had died while giving birth to Sally. Sally's father was in and out of prison because he refused to accept segregation as his birthright. After dating for a while, Osie and Sally decided to get married. Osie asked Sally's grandmother if Sally could be his wife. Sally's grandmother gave her blessings and not long afterward Osie and Sally were married. Osie was seventeen and Sally was fifteen when they were married.

Osie was one of the finest farmers in Alabama. Now that he had Sally at his side who also grew up farming, he felt like a king. Their first three children were girls and Osie worked them on the farm like they were men. One of his favorite sayings was "an idle mind is the devil's workshop." So, Mae, Minnie, and Kate worked extremely hard on the farm. From the union of Osie and Sally came fourteen children, six daughters and eight sons. This story is about the seventh son, Dal.

Dal was the eleventh child and the seventh son born to Osie and Sally. He was born on January 25, 1945. Dal never use his right hand as a baby. Everyone thought that he was naturally left-handed, but his right hand had been damaged during the birthing process. By the time Sally realized that Dal's right upper body was damaged, it was too late to do anything because the wrist, elbow, and shoulder was set in the wrong position. Back then, the doctors knew nothing about breaking bones and fusing them back together or replacing joints artificially.

As Dal grew from year to year, Osie and Sally noticed something different about him. He was independent, inquisitive, and had a kind of quiet indomitable spirit within him. Dal learned to do everything his other seven brothers did despite his right arm. He could jump higher, run faster, wrestle better than most of the boys his age. At the age of six, Dal was doing a full day's work on the farm alongside of his other siblings.

Dal always seemed to be preoccupied with doing things the right way. He possessed a keen sense of justice. While in elementary school, Dal and the other students would be given an aptitude test each year. One question that always appeared on the questionnaire was, "What do you want to be when you grow up?" Dal's answer was always the same, "preacher." He was unaware that Sally had earnestly prayed that God would anoint one of her sons to preach the gospel of Jesus Christ.

Osie was Baptist born and Baptist bred. Sally was Methodist. Sometimes Dal would go to the Methodist church with Sally, but most of the time, the family attended the St. James Baptist Church where Osie was one of the deacons. Dal hated sitting on the hard pews at St. James Baptist Church every Sunday morning. He would move from hip to hip, left to right and right to left throughout the Sunday School and morning worship service. When the congregation sang hymns, Dal did not understand why they held the notes so long. Sometimes they held the notes so long that Dal would lose the meaning the hymn was supposed to convey to the worshipper. Dal tried to sing along with the congregation, but he could not seem to keep time with the notes. When they would sing "A Charge to Keep I Have," they would be singing Cha—rge, and Dal would be singing "A God to Glorify." Osie and Sally made sure Dal went to church every Sunday, but he never felt any type of self-fulfillment at the Baptist church. It was as if he was involved in a ritual that lacked meaning for his life. Dal guessed that he had not received the new birth yet, or he was not old enough to understand what was going on or why it was going on.

When Dal was about four years old, a very significant event happened in his small hometown of Sulligent, Alabama. A Pentecostal-holiness preacher showed up and began preaching the gospel of Jesus Christ under a brush harbor. Men, women, boys, and girls traveled from miles around the small town of Sulligent to hear Elder Robert W. McDaniel preach the gospel of Jesus Christ. Elder McDaniel had a reddish complexion with reddish hair and his eyes danced like an albino's eyes. He had walked and thumbed his way from Jasper, Alabama, to Sulligent. He said that the Holy Spirit told him to come to Sulligent and preach the gospel of Jesus, the Christ, concerning the kingdom of God. His clothes were dusty, tattered, and well worn. His shoes were worn with holes in the soles. Elder McDaniel was a very charismatic speaker. When he preached, people would run to the altar to be saved and receive the gift of the Holy Ghost. They would speak in tongues and praise God with all their might. Two of Dal's older sisters got saved and received the Holy Ghost. Dal's mother went to the revival meeting and got saved, but his dad would not allow her to go back to the revival because people were saying that the preacher and those with him were throwing some kind of potion on the people. When women would fall to the floor under the anointing of the Holy Ghost, the missionaries would place a piece of cloth or other clothing over their legs to prevent anyone from seeing under their clothes. Those who were there to observe what was happening did not understand, so they started the rumor that the worshippers were wrapping themselves in sheets and rolling across the floor. The public began calling the Pentecostal-holiness people Holy-rollers. Instead of wounding the church, the rumors caused more people to come to church to see for themselves. The Sulligent Church of God in Christ started under a brush harbor, moved to a tent, and eventually built a church building. Many people were happy, but many were also unhappy, Particularly, the Baptist, because their members were leaving their churches in droves and flocking to the Pentecostal-holiness churches.

Dal's dad was Baptist, and he would not allow his mother to return to the Pentecostal-holiness Church after she went to the altar there and got saved. She was saved and sanctified, but she had not received the baptism of the Holy Ghost. Sally did not fight or disobey Osie. She stayed away from the Pentecostal-holiness Church as he asked her to do, but she kept on praying for the Holy Ghost right there at home. One night she was on her knees praying, earnestly seeking the baptism of the Holy Ghost. Suddenly, the Holy Ghost came upon her, and she fell to the floor and began speaking in tongues and praising God. This frightened Osie. He ran through house shouting, "chilluns, chilluns, what's wrong with your mama." Dal's dad was momentarily afraid, but his mother was just fine. She had been baptized in the Holy Ghost.

After this experience, Dal's dad allowed his mother to attend the Pentecostal-holiness church every Sunday with all the children. Because the Pentecostal-holiness churches usually held services longer than the other churches, Osie required Sally to cook and serve breakfast, prepare dinner, and oversee the cleaning of the kitchen before going to Sunday School. Sally did this with such dedication that Osie had nothing to disagree about relative to her church attendance. It was here in the Pentecostal-holiness church that Dal would be taught the real meaning of salvation and the existence and purpose of the Holy Ghost.

The Church of God in Christ (C.O.G.I.C.) was more interactive than most other churches. C.O.G.I.C. allowed musical instruments in worship that you did not dare use in the more traditional churches. The traditional churches used the piano and organ for worship. C.O.G.I.C. used guitars, drums, tambourines, trumpets, trombones, and even forks, rubboards, and spoons. C.O.G.I.C. members sang, clapped their hands, and danced in praise and worship services. At least once a week C.O.G.I.C. would have a tarrying service. In this service, seekers would go to the altar to call on Jesus and praise God as they waited expectantly for the Holy Ghost to indwell them. People would overfill the church trying to see someone receive the gift of the Holy Ghost. People would be standing on the back pews, others would be in the doors and windows, all waiting to see the manifestation of the Holy Ghost.

Dal accepted Jesus Christ as his personal savior at the age of twelve. Sometimes, Dal would go to the gravel pit alone and preach to the trees and hills. He was too shy to acknowledge his call to the gospel ministry at this age although he had known since the age of four that he would be a gospel preacher. These trips to the gravel pit continued over a period of two years. No one knew about these trips except Dal and his God. At the gravel pit, Dal would preach to his audience, (i.e.) the hills and trees as he imitated Elder R.W. McDaniel, the pastor of the Sulligent C.O.G.I.C. He would sing and pray as he worshiped his God in a way that he was ashamed to do in church.

Dal went to the altar every week to tarry for the gift of the Holy Ghost. He was determined not to be a hypocrite. He had observed others who was slain in the Spirit as they received the Holy Ghost. He had observed some who were pretending to be what they were not. Others came to the altar for reasons other than receiving the Holy Ghost. There was one young man who came to the altar because he wanted to marry one of the young women who had received the baptism of the Holy Ghost. C.O.G.I.C. taught that its members should only marry within C.O.G.I.C. because it would be very difficult to live holy and uphold C.O.G.I.C. doctrine if you were unequally yoked together with unbelievers. This young man fell out on the floor, danced, clapped his hands, and acted like he had really given his life to God. He continued this until he and the young lady got married. Afterward, he left the church and only showed up every now and then as a spectator. Dal was determined to be honest with himself and with God. He listened to peers in school tell jokes about preachers, they laughed and sometimes he laughed with them, but in his heart, he knew that he, too, was destined to be a preacher.

On a Saturday night in June 1959, Dal and a host of other young people were on the altar tarrying for the gift of the Holy Ghost. Dal would always be one of the last to go to the altar because there was one girl who would foam from the mouth as she called on Jesus. Dal would wait until she was seated at the altar, then he would go to the altar as far away from her as possible. She would foam from her mouth and then start slinging her head from side to side, and that foam from her mouth would be flying all over the place. If she was at one side of the altar, Dal would go to the opposite side of the altar. On this night, after Dal was seated, for some unexplained reason, the pastor started rearranging the seating. When he was finished, this girl was seated right next to Dal. Dal did not like this arrangement, but he was on the altar now, determined to receive the gift of the Holy Ghost. The pastor instructed Dal and the other seekers to stay focused on Jesus no matter what. He said that sometimes when the Holy Ghost was about to manifest itself the devil would do something to distract you such as, causing your skin to itch. If you stopped seeking Jesus to scratch, you might miss the blessing of the Holy Ghost. When the Holy Ghost comes into a place, He blesses and indwells those who are focused and waiting expectantly.

Dal and the other seekers started calling Jesus as they waited for the Holy Ghost to manifest itself and indwell them. Dal was focused more than ever before, but it was not long before the girl next to him was foaming from her mouth and slinging her head from side to side. Dal tried not to think about the fact that this girl was sitting next to him. He remembered what the pastor had said before the tarrying service began. Dal continued to call on Jesus with all his heart. He forgot about the girl sitting next to him. Dal heard a voice from deep down inside of him say "stand up." Dal answered to himself, "no way, not in front of all of these people." The voice spoke again, "stand up." Dal answered again to himself, "no way, not in front of all of these people." About this time, Dal felt apiece of the girl's foam slap him across the face. He wanted to stop and clean his face, but he remembered the pastor's admonition. Dal was determined not to allow Satan to win this time. Dal focused harder to push the girl next to him out of his mind. He got lost in his desire to be baptized in the Holy Ghost. Dal began to talk to God in his spirit. He said, "God, if that was really you telling me to stand up, tell me once again and I will do it." Immediately, the voice spoke from deep down on the inside, "stand up." Dal started to get up, but something took over Dal's body, mind, and spirit. His mouth was shouting praises to God and his body was moving in praise to God. Dal had surrendered his total being to God and as a result, the Holy Ghost made its abode within his body.

Dal had seen other seekers come under the anointing of the Holy Spirit, but now he understood it from the seeker's point of view. When Dal went across the floor praising God and then was knocked to the floor by the Holy Spirit, it was as if he was floating through the air. From a spectator's point of view, when a seeker is knocked to floor by the Holy Ghost, it looks as if they would be hurt bad, but from a participant's perspective, it is like a feather floating to the floor.

Dal came to himself speaking with other tongues and magnifying the God of Glory. Then he began to preach from St. Matthew 7:13-14, "Enter ye in at the strait gate: for wide is the gate, and broad is the way, that leadeth to destruction, and many there be which go in there at: Because strait is the gate, and narrow is the way, which leadeth unto life, and few there be that find it." Dal preached for about ten minutes. Then he heard the pastor say, "Can anyone deny that this young man has been anointed to preach the gospel of Jesus Christ. He has already preached his trial sermon." Dal was fourteen years old when he formally acknowledged his call to the ministry of Jesus Christ. As Dal contemplated his experience of the Holy Ghost indwelling him, he finally understood the full meaning of the words of the C.O.G.I.C. anthem, "You cannot join it, you've got to be born in it. This is the Church of God in Christ." Dal felt like a new person all over. His skin felt new. He reached up to wipe the girl's foam from his face, but it was already gone. Dal's skin felt like a newborn baby's skin. He had never experienced anything like this before. It was unexplainable. Dal knew that this was the beginning of a new life for him. "Behold, old things are passed away, all things are become new." Dal was determined to walk worthy of his new vocation. A total of fourteen young boys and girls had been baptized in the Holy Ghost. Their ages ranged from nine to fourteen.

Dal and the other young people in the Sulligent C.O.G.I.C. were very fortunate because their pastor, Elder Robert W. McDaniel, allowed them regular opportunities to exercise their various spiritual gifts. Dal preached and sang often. Other young people sang and read poetry. Elder McDaniel allowed Dal to organize a young people's inspirational hour every Sunday afternoon before Y.P.W.W. The Young People's Willing Workers (Y.P.W.W.) convened every Sunday evening from six to seven o'clock. Sometimes Dal would preach, and at other times he would have young aspiring missionaries teach. Dal always ended these services with a tarrying service to help the young seekers receive that baptism of the Holy Ghost. At one of these early services, there was a sudden sound from heaven and the Holy Ghost filled the sanctuary and the young people began speaking in other tongues and praising God. Many of them were baptized in the Holy Ghost. When Elder McDaniel and the adults arrived for Y.P.W.W., the young people were rejoicing and praising God, and speaking with other tongues as the spirit gave the utterance. Bodies were slain in the spirit all over the sanctuary, Elder McDaniel told the adults, "Don't stop them, join them." Dal's lifelong friend, Murray, had received the baptism of the Holy Ghost along with many other youths of the church.

Dal's ministry continued to grow in wisdom and faith as God used him among the youth at the Sulligent C.O.G.I.C. Members of the community began to call him "the boy preacher." He had no formal training in theology, but he had the Holy Ghost abiding within him on which he relied heavily for his understanding of scripture. Dal also benefitted from Elder McDaniel's sound teaching. He really taught and upheld the doctrine of the Church of God in Christ and the Bible. When Elder McDaniel was teaching and preaching, Dal listened actively, taking in every word. Elder Mac, as Dal and the members of the church fondly called him, taught Dal to always base his preaching on the holy scriptures contained in the Bible rather than on theological philosophies that sometimes-contradicted Biblical teachings as well as other theologies. Dal was taught that, as long as C.O.G.I.C. held that the Bible was the infallible written Word of God, the C.O.G.I.C. preachers must rightly divide the Old and New Testaments and live what they preached.

Dal studied his Bible with zeal. He read it from Genesis to Revelations several times and ran a parallel with the Bible and secular history. He often withdrew to solitary places so that he could study and meditate on Biblical Scriptures. He was obedient to the scripture that says, "Study to show yourselves approved unto God; a workman that needeth not to be ashamed, rightly dividing the Word of Truth." Dal had been asked to preach once before unexpectedly and found himself unprepared. From that day forward, Dal determined never again to be caught unprepared to preach the gospel of Jesus Christ. One of his favorite scriptures was "Be always ready to give an answer to any man that ask you a reason of the hope that lies within you." Dal did not utterly cast theology aside, but he carefully ran parallels between scripture and theology and accepted only that theology that agreed with scripture rightly divided. Dal sought to please God in all aspects of his life so that he would be able to walk worthy of the vocation to which he had been called, namely, preaching the gospel of Jesus Christ.

Elder McDaniel sensed that Dal had an incredibly special relationship with God. He observed and encouraged Dal as he grew in wisdom and scriptural knowledge. He gave Dal many opportunities to exercise his multifaceted ministry. Dal took full advantage of every opportunity in his quest to learn and preach the true gospel of Jesus, the Christ. When Dal interpreted scripture, it was as if he was looking at the entire Bible at once. He never interpreted a scripture in a way that would contradict another scripture. He possessed the ability to see things in scripture that others seemed afraid to contemplate.

Elder McDaniel not only served as the pastor of the Sulligent C.O.G.I.C., but he was also the District Superintendent of the Jasper-Sulligent District. The District Meetings always lasted for seven days with the Official Day on Sunday. Elder McDaniel allowed Dal to organize a Youth Inspirational Hour before Y.P.W.W. on Official Day of the District Meeting. Sometimes, Dal would preach and at other times he would invite other young ministers or missionaries to preach or teach. At one of these youth services, Dal took his text from the ninth chapter of St. John. His subject was "I was Blind, but Now I See." Dal and the district youth conducted a service that was so anointed that the heavens opened, and the Spirit was poured out on all that was present. When the service started, only the youth were there. But, once Dal started preaching and the anointing filled the sanctuary, all of the adults rushed back into the sanctuary to see who was preaching such a dynamic sermon. The adults could be heard saying, "That boy preaches like an old, seasoned preacher." Dal never allowed his success or his anointing and his many spiritual gifts to go to his head. When Dal prayed, he could always be heard saying, "Lord, keep me meek and humble." When he was finished ministering to the people, he always got on his knees and gave God the glory. He never seemed to think about himself. He was always concerned about the other person.

Dal's mother had prayed that God would anoint one of her sons to preach the Gospel of Jesus Christ. She told Dal that she had so prayed. Dal told his mother, "I have to preach the Gospel of Jesus Christ because I am a chosen vessel. Whatever else I do, I will always be a Gospel preacher." Dal's mom smiled and pondered all these things in her heart. She had known from birth that Dal was a special child.

Dal's tenth grade teacher, Mr. Bowman, had nothing good to say about Pentecostal-holiness churches. Dal entered his history class as one of the top students in the class. Once Mr. Bowman knew that Dal was a member of the Pentecostal-holiness church in Sulligent, he made sure he degraded the Sulligent C.O.G.I.C., whenever the word religion came up in history class. He would make fun of the way the Pentecostal- holiness churches praised and magnified God in their worship services. He called the saints who had been slain in the Spirit, "holy rollers." The word had gotten out, mistakenly, that the Pentecostal-holiness worshipers wrapped up in sheets and rolled across the sanctuary floor. Mr. Bowman had no understanding of the Pentecostal-holiness church. He had no idea that what happened in the upper room on the Day of Pentecost was still happening in the world today and would continue to take place over and over again wherever there are people who seek the indwelling power of the Holy Ghost. While other denominations taught that the Pentecostal experience was just for those in the upper room on the Day of Pentecost. C.O.G.I.C. taught as Peter said, "It is for you and your children, and your children's children, and even as many as the Lord, our God shall call." While other denominations stopped at the new birth and water baptism, C.O.G.I.C. taught that after being saved, (believing on the Lord Jesus and accepting him as your personal savior), being born again (the working of the Holy Spirit within), and being baptized in water, there remained the indwelling of the Holy Ghost within the human body as down payment on the glory that is to come with the appearing of our savior, Jesus Christ. Mr. Bowman did not understand the reaction of the human body, spirit, soul, and intellect to the indwelling presence of the Holy Ghost. Dal listened to Mr. Bowman continue his rage of insensitivity and ignorance about how Pentecostal-holiness people worshiped God. Dal never became angry or disrespectful toward Mr. Bowman. He knew that it was not possible to understand the indwelling power of the Holy Ghost until you experienced it firsthand. Jesus said it best in St. John's Gospel, "the world cannot receive this [gift]; the world cannot see it." One day, while the history class was studying world religions, Mr. Bowman started his tirade about how Pentecostal-holiness people wrapped up in sheets and rolled across the floor trying to get a reaction from Dal. Dal said nothing. Mr. Bowman continued his tirade against Pentecostal-holiness churches. Finally, he became bold enough to ask Dal if he still belonged to the "sanctified church" on the hill. Dal answered boldly, courageously, and unashamedly, "Of course, Jesus is real." At this point, the whole class told Mr. Bowman to leave Dal alone, and if he refused, they would deal with him. After this most of the harassment ceased. To Dal, this was a firsthand testimony of how God uses others to intercede for those who belong to him (those in the household of faith). This experience really encouraged Dal and helped to solidify his faith in the Lord Jesus Christ.

Elder McDaniel was a great preacher and teacher. Whatever he taught, he always supported with scripture. He taught Dal to never surrender his interpretation of the scripture until he was proven wrong with Biblical Scripture rightly divided. When some of the elderly saints taught that it was a sin to participate in sports, Elder McDaniel explained to Dal that it was not a sin to participate in sports. But, since many of the elderly members thought that it was, he asked Dal and the other youth not to participate in organized sports for the sake of the elderly members. Dal learned from scriptures that partying and drinking hard liquor was sinful. So, Dal did not attend worldly parties. When Dal's classmates would organize parties to raise funds for various school projects, Dal would contribute the price of admission, but he would not attend the party. Dal did not like to separate from his school peers, but he wanted to be sure that he was obedient to the word of God as revealed in the Bible. Dal remained friends with many of his classmates, but when they would head to the honky-tonk or beer joint, Dal would immediately part company. It was easy to see that Dal and some of his peers were traveling on completely different roads concerning spiritual things, yet they remained friends.

Many times, Dal had to stand alone, because most of the youth who had received the baptism of the Holy Ghost would backslide when school opened in August and get reclaimed after school closed in May. They did this every year so that they could attend the school parties and dances without being condemned. Openly backsliding was preferred by the youth rather than being hypocritical. Their reasoning was that if they backslid, the members of the church and the community would not expect them to uphold the way of holiness in their everyday lives. One day Dal and his friend M.J. was seriously considering backsliding so that they could participate in sports and attend the school sponsored parties and dances, but as they entered their homeroom during lunch, they heard their teachers say one to another, "There is something different about Dal and M.J. They are not like the other students. They do not swear or gamble. There's something about them that we don't see in the other students." Dal and M.J. was in the area called the cloakroom and had not come into view of the teachers yet. So, they looked at each other and said, "Man! We can't go back now!" The teachers never knew that Dal and M.J. overheard their conversation. Dal and M.J. left that room more determined than ever to live up to and uphold the principles of holiness. Those teachers' comments saved Dal and M.J. from backsliding. Sometimes, Dal's fellow students would test his faith by taunting him or jesting with him to see if they could make him become angry or fight. Dal always held firm to behavior becoming to holiness. It seemed that God's grace was always present to deliver Dal. When the girls would raise their skirts or dresses to tempt Dal or get a reaction from him, dal would say, "God bless you", and walk away. It was not easy to do, but Dal wanted to please God above all things.

When Dal was in the eleventh grade, a new teacher, and sports coach was hired at his school. His name was Mr. Black. He had just graduated from Miles College in Birmingham. He taught English and Biology in addition to coaching football, basketball, and track. Mr. Black was from the city and did not understand that the first two weeks of school many of the students helped their parents harvest their crops before they came to school. On Dal's first day in school that year, Mr. Black gave a biology test which Dal failed quite handsomely. He did not know that Dal was one of the top students in class. So, when Dal scored a big 100 on his next biology test, Mr. Black asked, "Who did you copy?" Dal answered, "I didn't copy, I just had time to study." Mr. Black did not believe Dal until the class affirmed that Dal was one of the top students in the class.

After being there a few months, Mr. Black began to observe how skilled Dal was on the football field and basketball court during physical education and recess. One day as he watched Dal and the other boys playing football during recess, his mouth flew open as he watched Dal running full speed into the end zone. Mr. Black was amazed by what he had just seen. Dal had almost no use of his right hand, and yet he could more than hold his own with the students with good use of both hands. Mr. Black wondered why Dal never tried out for the football or basketball teams. He knew from physical education classes that only one student could run faster than Dal and none had his endurance. Finally, one day in class, Mr. Black asked Dal why he never tried to make the school's football or basketball teams. Dal's answer was, of course, from a religious perspective. He explained that for the sake of the elderly members in his church, he had chosen not to play organized football or basketball. In a few minutes, the English class had become a Bible study class. Mr. Black and the students queried Dal on everything from why he did not attend the school parties to why sanctified girls did not wear lipstick or short shorts. With the help of the Holy Ghost, Dal answered every question with scriptural reference. Dal was so charismatic in his oratory that several of the students began to cry and say, "We want what you have." Dal explained to them how to be saved and receive the Baptism of the Holy Ghost. From that day forward at Lamar County Training School, both teachers and students showed extraordinary respect for Dal. They now understood that what Dal possessed in his body, spirit, and soul was more than just a fad, it was truly a way of life.

After Dal was promoted to the twelfth grade, his family moved to Denver, Colorado. Dal would have to finish his last year of high school in Denver. Dal lived in the district where he had to attend Manual High School. Manual High had about three thousand students in grades ten through twelve. The facility had three floors and a basement, two gyms, two swimming pools, and a football stadium with a quarter mile track. Dal had never seen a school this large and with these many students before. When Dal registered for school at Manual High, the dean told him that he would be placed in the eleventh grade because the standards at Manual High were higher than they were at the segregated colored schools in the South. Dal had been promoted to the twelfth grade and he did not want to repeat grade eleven. Suddenly, something clicked in Dal's mind. He remembered Mrs. Ruby Todd had told them back in Alabama that if they ever moved away and the new school wanted to move them back a grade, that they should ask to take a placement test. So, Dal asked the dean to allow him to be tested to determine his grade placement. The dean agreed to test Dal, but he warned Dal that if he scored lower than grade eleven, he would have to be placed further back than grade eleven. He told Dal that his A's and B's from the colored school in Alabama was only equivalent to C's and D's in the Denver Public Schools. Dal was determined to pass the placement test. He had an older sister back in Alabama, who was married, and Dal had decided that if he did not pass the test, he would return to Alabama and live with her until he graduated from high school. When Dal arrived at the cafeteria to be tested the next day, he was surprised to see the cafeteria full of students who had chosen to take the placement test to determine their grade placement. When the proctors passed out the test booklets and Dal recognized the C.B.A.T. (California Battery Achievement Test), he knew that he would score well on it. At Dal's old school back in Alabama, every student was required to take the C.B.A.T. every year to determine their academic growth. Dal had passed the C.B.A.T. every year scoring above his grade level each year. When Dal had taken the test in Alabama, he was under time constraints, but because it was to determine his grade placement in school, he was under no time constraints this time. A few days after the C.B.A.T. had been administered, the dean called Dal into his office. He asked, Who did you copy?" Dal looked at the dean and said, "If you had really looked at my records from Alabama as you indicated you had, you should have seen my scores for this same test for grades seven through eleven. If you would like for me to retest, I will take the test again with you watching me." The dean looked intently at Dal and said, "Dal, we can't move you back. If you were not already a senior, we would have to skip you forward." The dean continued, "You scored at the college level in every area except language. Your language score is 11.9 which is the beginning of twelfth grade." Dal was pleased that he had scored well on the C.B.A.T.

In Denver, Dal, his mother, his younger sister, and brother attended the Bibleway Church of God in Christ where Elder Sims was the pastor. It was small and homey, and reminded them of the church back in Sulligent, Alabama. Elder Sims had moved to Denver from Texas with his family. He took Dal under his tutelage and taught him what he knew about expository preaching. Dal listened and took his advice. Elder Sims taught Dal not to use too many fill-ins while speaking to the congregation. Dal joined the choir and the Young Ministers Association.

One Sunday afternoon, Dal and about five other young ministers were scheduled to preach at an evangelistic service. Dal was the only one that was really "young in age". The others were young in the ministry but, were in their late twenties or thirties relative to age. The association officers did not know anything about Dal because he was new there. So, Dal was scheduled to speak first because of his age. Dal preached from the Book of Acts. His text was, "Except you Abide in the Ship, You Cannot be Saved." When he was finished, the entire congregation was standing and praising God. The next speaker was introduced, and he came to the podium singing a son entitled, "Jesus Said, Believe on Me." He was very obese. At the least, he must have weighed between three and four hundred pounds. He sang until people were dancing and singing all over the church. He ran down one aisle and up another. Suddenly, something happened that was both comical and frightening at the same time. This young minister had completely exhausted himself before he had a chance to take his text. While he was running down the aisle, he did not have the energy to get back to the pulpit, so he sat down in the back of the church on someone's lap because all of the pews were filled. The person he sat on was trying to stay calm, but the weight was too much. He began to shout, "Get up! Get up!" And…young people will be young people! The members of the youth choir where Dal was sitting were all down between the pews laughing. Dal wanted to laugh with them, but his mother caught his eye and shook her head. When the young minister finally made it back to the pulpit, he could hardly speak. He mumbled something about he had prepared a sermon, but he could not preach it now. He was too exhausted to speak. Dal was quite surprised because he had not expected such a bombastic beginning to end with a whimper. Dal reflected on the plight of this young minister and the embarrassment he must have felt. He was glad that he had been taught how to minister to the congregation.

Dal lived in Denver for one year and graduated from Manual High School in 1963. He worked as a house man at a country club of about one month before deciding to return to Alabama and become an evangelist. Dal had no choice because the spirit of God was upon him to preach the gospel of Jesus Christ. As soon as Dal arrived back in Alabama, Elder McDaniel told Dal that it would be appropriate for him to conduct his first full revival at the Sulligent Church of God in Christ where he grew up. Dal asked his friend Murray to provide the music for the revival. Dal was a good, charismatic speaker and an accomplished singer, and Murray was an excellent guitarist.

The next week Dal started a revival that would last for one month and would shake the foundations of the community of Sulligent and the surrounding area. Dal was ready. He had prayed and fasted for many days that God would anoint him and let his word convict the hearts of men, women, boys, and girls. Dal sang, preached, prayed for the sick and afflicted, and worked with those on the altar until perspiration sounded like water in his shoes. The altar was overflowing every night. When Dal sang, "Something got a Hold to Me," people would enjoy his singing so much that they would send five, ten, and twenty dollar bills by the usher with a request asking Dal to sing another song. One night as Dal arrived at church, he overheard a young woman say to another person, "There's nothing to that, those people are just pretending. It is not real. Watch me get in the prayer line tonight to prove it." When Dal invited the worshippers for prayer, this young woman got in the prayer line. When Dal laid his hands on her, he wanted God to reveal Himself to her. He wanted God to show her that He was real. But he was reluctant to speak because he had overheard her conversation earlier, and he did not want self to get in the way of God's purpose. He wanted to pray the prayer of faith according to the will of God and not the will of Dal. But the Holy Ghost forced the words out of Dal's mouth, "Lord, show her that its real."

The Holy Ghost knocked the young woman to the floor. Then he would allow her to get to her feet and knock her down again. This happened several times until one of the members who was not in the spirit reached out and touched her to pick her up and broke the connection between this woman and the work of the Holy Ghost. Dal knew that the Holy Ghost was in charge of this revival. The Holy Spirit was convicting the hearts of men, women, boys, and girls from all over western Lamar County, Alabama. The elderly who had called Dal, "The Boy Preacher," those who had attended school with Dal, and the younger generations who had heard of him were being saved, sanctified, and baptized in the Holy Ghost. People were being healed from various diseases and illnesses.

Dal prayed for those who had needs other than being baptized in the Holy Ghost first. Then the altar would be prepared for those who sought the baptism of the Holy Ghost with the pray warriors, musicians, and singers who would tarry with them until the Holy Ghost would fill the sanctuary and indwell those who were ready in the power and fullness of Jesus' joyous peace. Sometimes those waiting for the Holy Ghost would receive it immediately. Others would tarry for hours before being baptized in the Holy Ghost. Still others would come for months and years before being baptized in the spirit. Dal knew one elderly man who tarried for more than twenty years before he finally received the Baptism of the Holy Ghost. The problem was that this elderly man was afraid of the Holy Ghost. He was afraid to give himself completely over to the will of God. Dal often observed the man during tarrying services. When the Holy Ghost would come upon him, he would catch hold of the pew and would not let go. He was visibly afraid to allow the Holy Ghost to indwell him. Dal understood why some people received the baptism of the Holy Ghost faster than others. He had observed that many of the worshippers came to the altar with preconceived notions about how they were going to act when they received the Holy Ghost. He understood that the quickest way to be filled with the Holy Ghost was through saying yes to God's complete will without reservation or hesitation.

One night, two fourteen-year-old young ladies came to the altar and surrendered their lives to God. Dal and the other youth of the church had been witnessing to them for several days. When they came to the altar, Dal could see that they were profoundly serious about giving their lives to Jesus. Sharon was reserved, while Beatrice was more emotional and expressive. They were from a multi-generational bootlegging family. Their parents and grandparents were involved in selling illegal alcoholic beverages in a dry county, and yet, here they were, on God's altar crying out for deliverance with all their tender, aching hearts. Beatrice's grandparents on the maternal side of her family were regular church going, respected members of the St. Andrews Baptist Church as well as respected members of the community.

Beatrice came to the altar and surrendered herself to God without reservation. Dal could see the Holy Ghost abiding upon her before she got to the altar. As soon as she started calling upon Jesus, the Holy Ghost overshadowed her. Just as she was about to speak in tongues, her mother came and took her from the altar. Beatrice left the altar with the spirit all over her. Her mother left trembling from the fear of God. Sharon remained on the altar and became saved and sanctified and continued to seek the baptism of the Holy Ghost. Sharon was on the altar each night seeking the indwelling power of God, but Beatrice's parents would not allow her to come to the altar. She came to church each night, but she was forced to sit in the rear of the sanctuary between her mother and grandmother. Despite this arrangement, when the spirit of God came into the sanctuary, Beatrice's hands would go up in praise to God. She would grab herself and look over at her mother and grandmother. She would shout praises to God, then grab her mouth. Dal could see the Holy Spirit all over Beatrice. He knew that she was a chosen soul and had to be delivered. Dal handpicked Murray, Gloria, Missionary Johnson-Hollis, and a few other spirit-filled saints who could be trusted to fast and pray together until God, in His wisdom, delivered Beatrice and baptized her in the Holy Ghost. The revival continued for another three weeks. The membership grew. The pews were filled to capacity and beyond, Dal and his spirit-filled group fasted and prayed every day for three weeks that God would deliver Beatrice and baptize her in the Holy Ghost. Dal did not know why Beatrice was dragged from the altar, or who was behind it, but he was more than confident that Jesus would loose her from the bonds of Satan so that she might praise Him in the beauty of holiness.

On the last day of the revival, Beatrice attended the revival with the freedom to come back to the altar if she so desired. She came to the altar and immediately was filled with the Holy Ghost and began to speak with other tongues as the spirit gave the utterance. Dal began to sing the song, "I Got Just What I Wanted From the Lord." The Spirit of God so filled the sanctuary that it appeared as if there was a cloud that filled the sanctuary, and the Holy Ghost began to indwell many of the worshippers who were on the altar. The joy of the Lord seemed to be manifesting itself inside and outside the sanctuary. People were being baptized in the Holy Ghost outside the sanctuary as well as inside the sanctuary. People were shouting praises to God everywhere. Dal dismissed the service while the people were still praising God, in the sanctuary, in the street, in the parking lot. The people were filled with the joy of the Lord. Beatrice left church leaping and praising God and dancing in praise to God for His deliverance. She had traffic backed up on Main Street on Friday night as she danced and praised God in the spirit. Dal began to shout, "The glory is thine Lord! The glory is thine! Glory to the Father and His Lamb!" Dal was doing as the Apostle Paul admonished in scripture, "Make full proof of your ministry. Do the work of an evangelist." His ministry had gotten off to a blessed start. When other pastors heard about how God had used

Dal in the Sulligent church, many of them scheduled Dal to conduct revivals for their churches. Many of their churches had no members or very few members. These were the churches who could not afford the well-known urban evangelists. Also, many of the urban evangelist refused to go to rural churches to conduct revivals. Dal possessed a different spirit. He was determined to preach wherever God opened the door. He went everywhere, to large urban churches filled to capacity. Or to small rural churches with no or few members.

Dal's next revival was in a small rural church in Berry, Alabama. The church had exactly three members, the pastor, his wife, and an aged church mother. Dal's friend, Murray, had found employment, but agreed to drive to Berry each night to provide music for the revival. The pastor also hired a young lady from the Methodist church to provide music for the revival. She turned out to be quite an accomplished pianist. She and Dal practiced together and sang duets and solos for the revival. The pianist's name was Ellen. She received the Holy Ghost during the first week of the revival and joined the church. People were being saved, sanctified, and filled with the Holy Ghost. Others were healed from various diseases, delivered from the bonds of Satan, and set free in the name of the Lord Jesus. When the word got out about how God was blessing folk, people came from all around the region to be blessed of God. Others came to see the glory of God manifested in the services. The altar was filled from the very first night. The people had a hunger and thirst for the salvation of God. They received the word of God from Dal gladly. Dal had been scheduled for one week, but the revival lasted for thirty days. Dal preached, prayed, sang, and tarried with the seekers every night for thirty days. Sometimes Dal worked so hard that every step he took during tarrying service and prayer the perspiration could be heard going swish, swish in his shoes. When the revival closed, more than forty people had received the gift of the Holy Ghost, and the altar was still overflowing with seekers. Dal gave

God the glory because he understood that he was merely an instrument in God's hands. It was not to be attributed to his greatness, but the work of the Holy Spirit that churches were being filled through his ministry. Dal could always be heard saying, "The glory is thine, Oh, God. The gory is thine."

When Dal arrived in Thomasville, Alabama, to conduct a revival, he had been an evangelist long enough to comprehend why many of the more established evangelists hardly ever went into the rural areas. The people in the rural areas did not have as much legal tender to give as their counterparts in the urban areas. What resources the rural people possessed they gave in abundance willingly and joyfully. While legal tender was given in the offerings in urban cities, sometimes in the rural areas the people gave canned food, meat (sometimes on the hoof), eggs, etc., from their resources. So the more established evangelists seem to have preferred the legal tender. This is not to say that the evangelists who did venture into the rural areas did not prefer legal tender over eggs, meat, and canned goods, but rather that they refused to leave the rural flocks unattended. Jesus told all of his true laborers to go into his vineyard and work and whatever is right he would pay. This is the attitude that Dal had always tried to exhibit in his ministry. He had seen God work wonders and miracles among the people in the rural areas, but the offering for the evangelist was low. Dal knew that God had anointed him as an apostle of evangelism, and he wanted to stay within his anointing.

The first night in Thomasville, a few worshippers arrived on time (7:30 p.m.). Most of the worshipper arrived late at about 8:30 p.m. The first night's attendance was about twenty-five worshippers. Dal preached as if the house was filled to capacity. At the end of the first night's service, Dal asked the prayer warriors to be at the church on time for the remainder of the revival so that prayer could start on time. Dal believed that time was important, and he did not like being late for anything. The Bible teaches that we should redeem the time. Dal did not like telling God that he would meet him for worship at one time and then show up an hour late. He had purposed in his heart that if the prayer warriors were not there on time, he would be there himself to start prayer on time each night. He reminded the worshippers that the time stated for the start of services was important and worship services should begin accordingly. The next night at 7:30 p.m., Dal and the few worshippers who were on time started service at 7:30 p.m. When Dal and the other worshippers got up from their knees and turned to face the congregation, they were surprised to see the sanctuary filled to capacity. Dal had prayed that God would fill the sanctuary to capacity during the revival, be he left it up to God how to do it. Yes, the posters and handbills were all over town, but it was still in God's hands. During testimonial service, the people began to tell how God had enabled them to hear Dal's entire sermon the night before as they rode in their cars, lay in their beds, or sat on their porches. God had somehow carried Dal's voice all over the region so that the people could hear his sermon for miles around. Therefore, they had come to the revival on this night to hear what thus says the Lord. Dal was amazed, but he gave God the praise, knowing that with God, all things are possible. When those habitually late worshippers arrived between eight and eight-thirty, there was nowhere to sit. They seemed surprised to see that Dal was already into his sermon.

During the prayer for deliverance and healing, a transient worker came for prayer. He suffered from acute bursitis in his feet that caused him severe pain so that he had to wear special shoes. Dal did not even lay hands on him but, told him to go to the sanctuary door seven times and he would be healed. The man obeyed Dal and on the seventh trip to the door something happened to him. He began to leap and shout in praise to God. He leaped so high that Dal thought his head would hit the ceiling. He testified that while obeying Dal's directive to go to the door of the sanctuary seven times his feet began to hurt so bad that he did not think he could make it, but he persevered for his healing. For the next two weeks the sanctuary was filled to capacity and men, women, boys, and girls were saved, sanctified, and filled with the Holy Ghost. Demons crying with loud voices came out of many. Others were healed from various diseases. When Dal left Thomasville, the altar was overflowing with seekers for the Holy Ghost, healing, and deliverance. God was confirming His word in Dal's ministry with signs and wonders, miracles, and gifts of the Holy Ghost.

After evangelizing for several years, Dal began to desire more material things, but never made enough money to acquire any of the things he wanted to buy. So Dal decided that he was not going to preach anymore. Dal did not know that God would deal with him so quickly. Immediately, God afflicted Dal's throat with something like strep throat. This affliction not only affected Dal's throat, but it took away his voice. Dal went to the doctor and took shots of antibiotics as well as antibiotic tablets. The antibiotics cleared up Dal's throat, but he still could not talk. Every time he tried to talk, it sounded like gargling noises. Dal would become angry because no one could understand him. The doctors checked Dal's throat more than once but, could find no reason he could not talk. When Dal went to God in prayer, he then understood why God had taken away his ability to speak. Dal confessed to God that he had decided not to preach anymore. God told Dal that he was a chosen vessel and that he had to preach the gospel of Jesus Christ. He could not just quit anytime he wanted. Dal began to cry yes to God's will and way. He cried, "My will serves you Jesus." This he said in his heart because he could not speak in a normal way. After he said yes to God, Dal's voice returned, and he began to praise God. His voice now seemed stronger and clearer than ever before. Dal now understood the difference between being called and being a chosen vessel. If you are called, you come if you want when you want, but when you are chosen by God, you really have no choice in the matter. You do what God tells you to do when He tells you to. Dal had learned an invaluable lesson; one he would never forget. Dal knew that he was born to preach. Dal had sung with choirs and quartets since he was twelve years old. In quartet singing, there was a high-pitched voice called, "the fifth." Dal was a natural tenor, or lead singer, but he had always wanted to sing in the fifth. His voice was too deep to reach the fifth. After God restored Dal's voice, he went to church and sang with his old choir that he had trained. He sang and praised God in song like never before. He even reached the fifth. Dal made a solemn vow to God that night. He vowed that he would never again attempt to put aside his ministry or his anointing. Dal now understood Jeremiah's statement relative to the anointing, "It's like fire shut up in my bones." Dal was indeed a fisher of men and God had chosen him to preach the gospel of Jesus Christ to all men everywhere. Ever since this experience, Dal does not worry about how much money he will receive, but he has taken Jesus at His word, "go into my vineyard and work, and whatever is right, I will pay." Dal's praise and prayer is always, "Not my will, but thine be done. My will serves you Lord."

When Dal returned to Sulligent, Elder McDaniel called him into his office and informed him that the jurisdictional Bishop wanted him to serve as jurisdictional chaplain for the state of Alabama. Dal accepted the position. He saw this as an opportunity to expand his service to the people. When the Jurisdictional Holy Convocation convened in Birmingham the following year, Dal was there to carry out his responsibilities as jurisdictional chaplain. At this time, the convocation lasted for ten days, and Dal was at his post every day and every night. He didn't own many suits, so he mixed and matched what he owned so that he wouldn't have to wear the same suit every day. Dal opened the worship services every day and night with singing and prayer. Oftentimes, he had to extend the praise and worship because jurisdiction officials were not yet on the pulpit. He soaked many shirts and jackets as he kept the services upbeat and lively while waiting for the officials to enter the sanctuary so that he could present the jurisdictional chairman. It was in this convocation that Dal got his first real induction into the workings of church politics. He had thought that he would at least receive enough of a stipend to pay for his convocation expenses. Dal watched as the other officials received stipends of three hundred, five hundred, and eight hundred dollars. To say the least, Dal was very disappointed, but there was a greater disappointment in this very same convocation. Dal had gone before the Ordination Committee to be ordained an Elder in the church only to be denied after passing their examination for ordination. Dal had his pastor's letter of recommendation in order, he answered more than ninety percent of the committee's questions correctly, and he was the only candidate who had done full time evangelism making full proof of his ministry. Still, Dal was denied ordination without being given a reason as to why he was denied. The committee had tried to unnerve Dal while he was before the committee being examined. Dal was seated in the middle of the floor with the committee forming a circle around him. There was nowhere to look except into the eyes of one of the committee members. When asked a question by one of the members regarding doctrine, Dal looked up to gather his thoughts when one of the committee members asked, "Why are you looking at the ceiling? Look at the chairman, he asked the question." Dal looked at the chairman and answered the question. Then Dal was asked an ambiguous question. "What is the gospel?" Dal said, "The gospel is the good news of eternal life through Jesus Christ." This answer was not what the committee was expecting to hear. They wanted Dal to quote Romans 1:16, " … it is the power of God unto salvation."

… When the licensed ministers were called to be ordained and blessed by the Bishop, Dal's name was not called. Yet Dal had performed better than the other candidates during the examination. The only reason Dal was given for not being ordained was that he was young and could wait to be ordained. Dal would learn the true reason why he was denied ordination by accident, or should we say an act of Providence. Toward the close of the convocation, as Dal walked down the corridor which separated the sanctuary from the conference rooms, he heard the assistant to the bishop and the jurisdictional chairman discussing he and his pastor, Elder McDaniel. Dal heard the chairman say, "Mac (short for McDaniel) and that boy down there in Sulligent, he doesn't need to be ordained, too much power down there together." Dal pondered their conversation in his heart, but he never told them he overheard their conversation concerning why they refused to ordain him.

After the convocation, Dal moved to Tennessee to work for his brother-in-law and his sister, Arcie. They operated a trucking business and a service station and wanted Dal to help them supervise the service station. Dal continued to evangelize the state of Tennessee. He joined the Eastern Tennessee Jurisdiction where the presiding Bishop was Bishop J.O. Patterson at the time. Eastern Tennessee held their convocation earlier than did Alabama. Do Dal decided to register for the Young Minister's Class and go before Eastern Tennessee's Ordination Board to be ordained. Dal passed the board's examination and was promptly ordained by Bishop J.O. Patterson on August 13, 1967. When Dal returned to Alabama to carry out his duties as jurisdictional chaplain the following week, most the of the Elders had already heard that he was ordained in Tennessee. The presiding Bishop, Bishop C.A. Ashworth, called Dal to his office and asked, "What are you doing with Tennessee ordination papers? You are an Alabama preacher. Give me those Tennessee papers, I'm giving you Alabama papers." Dal asked Bishop Ashworth to allow him to keep his Tennessee papers because of their sentimental value, Bishop Ashworth consented and presented Dal with his Alabama credentials.

While living in Tennessee, Dal and his friend, Elder Felton Smith preached together as Evangelists. Dal and Smith traveled to Panama City, Florida to conduct a revival for Elder McCleod. God came in and blessed the worshippers through signs and wonders, might acts, and gifts of the Holy Ghost. There was one member there who had five children, each of whom had been fathered by different evangelists who had conducted revivals there. Dal and Smith started prayer three times a day. They prayed earnestly that God would loose the bound and set the captives free from the bondage of Satan. Elder McCleod was very fearful that the member with the children would entrap Dal and Smith. However, Dal and Smith kept the young woman in prayer and never allowed her to be alone with either of them. One morning during the nine o'clock prayer Dal and Smith noticed that the Holy Spirit was working within the young woman. She got up from prayer and headed toward the rear exit to leave the prayer service. Dal and Smith quickly exited the front and met her at the rear exit and persuaded her to remain for the duration of the prayer service. Dal and Smith continued to pray that God through Jesus Christ would set the woman free from the bonds of Satan. During the evening service, the woman was slain in the spirit and began to speak with other tongues as the spirit gave the utterance. The power of God was manifested in that church as people were healed of various diseases, demons came out of many, and gifts of the Holy Ghost was given. At the end of the service, Elder McCleod called the young lady to the front of the congregation and confessed that he had promised the woman a complete set of clothes from head to toe if she ever got saved and received the Holy Ghost. He said, "Thank God that she has received the gift of the Holy Ghost! Her salvation is worth much more than clothes." The whole church went up in praise to God. What a joy to see God's little ones set free from the shackles of sin.

Shortly after the Panama City Revival, Dal and Smith parted company on the evangelistic trail, but remained life-long friends. Smith remained in Tennessee and Dal moved to Cleveland, Ohio.

In Cleveland, Dal joined the Saintes Temple C.O.G.I.C. where his older sister, Minnie attended. Dal sang with the choir and preached often while at Saints Temple. One night during worship service, the Holy Spirit instructed Dal to prophesy concerning the Saints Temple C.O.G.I.C. Dal quenched the spirit because he did not want to say what the Spirit had instructed him to say. Dal left Saints Temple Church and began attending the 110th Street C.O.G.I.C. He wanted to make sure that what he had been instructed to say was from the Holy Spirit and not from some other source. No matter how hard Dal tried to get away from the prophesy, it kept coming back to him. Dal couldn't sleep at night. He worried every day as to whether or not he was being disobedient to the Holy Spirit. Fear seized Dal because he knew that if he did not proclaim the prophesy and someone died in their sin as a result of him not delivering the prophesy their blood would be required at his hands in judgement. Finally, after several weeks, as Dal prayed and meditated in the Spirit, he spoke to the Lord and said, "God, if this is really you telling me to prophesy concerning the Saints Temple C.O.G.I.C., tell me again right now." Immediately, an audible voice spoke in Dal's ear that left no doubt that this was really the Holy Spirit instructing Dal to prophesy concerning Saints Temple C.O.G.I.C. Dal had never experienced anything like this before or since. An audible voice spoke one word into Dal's ear with such force and conviction that Dal's ear trembled and vibrated for many days. The voice said, "Go." It was not a bombastic voice nor a loud voice. It was a very soft voice with such a force and power that it was heard deep down in Dal's inner ear. This was the first time Dal had ever heard the voice of God audibly, and it was an experience that he would never forget. Dal returned to the Saints Temple C.O.G.I.C. at the first opportunity to prophesy as the Holy Spirit had instructed him. It was a weeknight worship service when the church gave Dal an opportunity to express himself toward the end of the service. Dal stood up and said, "The Spirit of the Lord says there is sin in the camp. If it is not confessed and stopped, the Holy Spirit is going to pass through this church and clean out the sin. I don't know what is going on or who is involved, but the Spirit says clean it up or else He will visit this church with judgment and not mercy." When Dal had finished prophesying, it seemed as if a huge weight lifted off his shoulders.

Immediately, the pastor stood up behind Dal and condemned him because of the prophesy. The pastor said, "The Holy Spirit really didn't instruct you to prophesy. Maybe you had an unction, but not according to knowledge." Dal looked intently at the pastor and told about why he had left the church to keep from prophesying. He told how the Holy Spirit wouldn't allow him to rest until he had delivered the prophesy. Several of the younger ministers got up and condemned Dal because of the prophesy. A few years later, while Dal was conducting a revival in Mobile, Alabama, one of the young ministers who had tried to condemn Dal because of the prophesy at the Saints Temple C.O.G.I.C., came to the revival. He came up to Dal and began begging forgiveness. Dal didn't even remember the incident nor the minister. He identified himself as one of the young ministers from Saints Temple C.O.G.I.C. He began to tell Dal about how the Holy Spirit had revealed how the pastor had been involved sexually with the church mother and how his wife had left him. He told Dal how the pastor's wife had wanted to come back home and how the pastor would not allow her to return. He told how the pastor had married a younger woman and how this caused the church mother to become mentally disturbed and leave her family for a time. Dal began to cry out to God for those who had not heeded his prophesy, asking God to have mercy on them. Dal found no glory because his prophesy had come to pass. He would much rather have had those involved repent and turn from their wickedness and be saved and filled with the Holy Ghost. To Dal, what the young minister said to him was proof that his prophesy was from the Lord. Dal knew that the only way to know whether or not a prophesy is from God is to see if it comes to pass.

During the decade of the 1960s, Dal's ministry was adversely affected by events taking place in the Church of God in Christ, after the death of the founder, Bishop Charles Harrison Mason. This period is usually referred to as the dark period in the history of C.O.G.I.C. The problem was a power struggle between the Bishop O.T. Jones, Sr., who had been duly elected as the senior Bishop of C.O.G.I.C and the Executive Board who assisted Bishop Mason in his final years. Dal tried to stay out of the conflict because he knew that it would have been impossible for him to be engaged in such a struggle and still be consecrated enough to meet the spiritual needs of the worshippers. When Dal would arrive at some churches for revivals, he would be asked by the pastor, "Who are you with, The Executive Board or Bishop O.T. Jones, Sr.?" Of course, Dal didn't know how to answer this question because he was not aware who these pastors supported. Dal would answer, "I'm trying to stay out of the conflict so that I can be free to preach in all of the churches." Dal's answer was never good enough. Some of the pastors would allow Dal to preach one night only, give him an offering, and send him on his way. Many revivals never took place and many souls were probably lost because of the power struggle within C.O.G.I.C.

While residing in the city of Cleveland, Dal entered Cuyahoga Community College and graduated with an Associate of Arts degree. During his studies at Tri-C, Dal tutored an older lady who had reared her family and returned to college to earn a degree. While tutoring her in math at her home, her husband often talked to Dal about religious topics and church doctrines. He told Dal about his son whom he had wanted to become a minister. His son had chosen another field of endeavor.

He asked Dal if he believed that the Sabbath was ordained of God and that it should be kept? Dal answered in the affirmative but, said that it would be impossible to go all the way back to the beginning of creation to determine which day one should rest or keep the Sabbath. Dal said, "The best one can hope to do as regarding the Sabbath is to keep the Sabbath one day out of seven." The deacon's eyes lit up like lamps as he proceeded to offer Dal the pastorate at the largest Seventh Day Adventist congregation in the city of Cleveland, Ohio. As it turned out, he was the Chief Deacon of the church. Dal told him he would have to pray about it before he could make a decision on the offer. The deacon told Dal that if he became their pastor, he could go to any suburb and pick any house he wanted; that he could go to any car lot and pick out any car he wanted. He stated that Dal, his spouse, and their children could attend any school (private or public) of their choice. Dal later discovered that the deacon was very wealthy and could easily afford all the things he had offered Dal. Dal thought about his offer and discussed it with his wife, Marlyn, and their children. Dal had grown up in the Pentecostal-Holiness church and all of his training had been in the C.O.G.I.C. He asked the deacon how his church felt about various teachings that were the foundation of the C.O.G.I.C. doctrine. The deacon told Dal that so long as he accepted the belief that one should keep the Sabbath, the other doctrinal points didn't matter. While Dal prayed and thought on the offer to become pastor of the Seventh Day Adventist church, the deacon continued to discuss scripture with Dal at every opportunity. When he would discuss scripture with Dal, the deacon seemed to be mesmerized by Dal's knowledge of scripture. The deacon made Dal the same offer at least three times. He again told Dal, "Choose your house, anywhere you want to live; choose the car you want to drive; you your wife, and your children can attend any college or university you choose. Don't worry about the price. Just be our pastor." Dal knew this was not an empty promise because the deacon was very wealthy. Dal pondered the offer for a couple of weeks and prayed about it. Dal began to talk to God about the offer as if he was talking to his father or mother while seeking advice on some very important decision. Dal said, "God, I have asked you to allow me to earn my doctorate in religious studies. I want my children to attend the college of their choice. I do need an automobile. I certainly need a house for my family. Dal again called a family meeting with his wife and children to get additional input from them because this was a major decision. After the meeting, Dal decided to meet with the deacon the next day to tell him that he had decided to accept his offer and become the pastor of the Seventh Day Adventist church. As Dal slept that night, he was awakened at 1:00 a.m. by the voice of God that said to him, "Do not accept the offer, I am going to bring about some changes COGIC that will be needed at a later time." The next day, Dal told the deacon that he could not accept the pastorate at the Seventh Day Adventist church. The deacon was disappointed, but Dal knew that his decision was the will of God.

After Dal graduated from Cuyahoga Community College, he relocated to Alabama. His anointing and his reputation for filling empty churches by allowing God to use the many gifts of the spirit in his fivefold ministry to heal, deliver, and set free many who were in bondage to Satan gave him favor with the pastors and jurisdictional leaders. Dal had booked nine months of revivals. However, there was much conflict going on in the jurisdiction. Dal later found out that the Jurisdictional Executive Board had attempted to oust the presiding Bishop. Their claim was that they wanted someone who was a native son of Alabama. The presiding Bishop lived in Ohio and wouldn't move to Alabama. Most of the pastors, ordained Elders, and licensed ministered favored Elder R.W. McDaniel, as a replacement as presiding Bishop. When Elder W.T. Humboldt, the assistant to the presiding Bishop, found out that he was not the choice for presiding Bishop, he went to the presiding Bishop and told everything. With this information, the presiding Bishop survived the attempted coup. After surviving the attempted coup, the presiding Bishop removed all of the Executive Board members who had taken part in the attempted coup and replaced them with younger Elders who had little leadership experience. This is the arena in which Dal found himself upon his return to Alabama. It was in this arena that his faith in God would be sorely tested.

These younger Elders had divided the jurisdiction into two camps. Their expectation was that every voting member of the jurisdiction would declare allegiance to one of the two camps but, no one would be allowed to stand neutral. Dal was approached by the leaders of both camps to join their group. He was told that one of them would be next presiding Bishop of the jurisdiction. Dal turned down the offers from both camps because he thought that joining one camp meant that he wouldn't be free to preach in the other camp. Dal's refusal to join either of the two camps caused both groups to begin persecuting him in an attempt to destroy his ministry. Within two weeks, Dal received telephone calls, postcards, and letters from the jurisdictional pastors who had scheduled him for revivals. Within two weeks, nine months of revivals had been cancelled. Within two weeks, Dal's entire livelihood, (full-time evangelism), was gone. Dal had no clue that Elders in the church could imagine such evil devices against one of their own. A few days later, the Holy Spirit showed Dal in a vision that the jurisdictional pastors had been told not to allow him to preach anywhere in the jurisdiction. No, this order did not come from the presiding Bishop, it came from those young pastors who had been appointed to executive positions in the jurisdiction who saw Dal as a threat to their jurisdictional ambitions. Dal decided to approach one of the older Elders who had watched him grow from an infant to adulthood in the Church of God in Christ. He had watched him grow from a novice to an experienced minister in the C.O.G.I.C. He had watched as the

Holy Ghost used Dal mightily in yearly revivals at his church. He and the pastor that Dal grew up under were nationally revered as the "Twin Preachers of Alabama." Dal went to him and asked, "Elder Tally, have you been told or pressured not to allow me to preach in the church where you are pastoring." The question hit him like a ton of bricks. The surprise and astonishment were written all over his face. After he gathered himself, he denied that he had been told not to allow Dal to preach in his pastorate. Dal related to him the vision that the Holy Ghost had revealed to him letting him know that the pastors had been told not to allow him to preach in the jurisdiction. During the following year a young Elder opened a church in the same town where Elder Tally was pastoring, and the young jurisdictional leaders decided that they wanted to promote him to District Superintendent. However, to do this, they would have to remove Elder Tally from the position. The presiding Bishop would not allow the young leaders to follow through with their plan. After having been persecuted by the young jurisdictional executives, Elder Tally, came to Dal and admitted that the pastors had been told not to allow Dal to preach anywhere in the state of Alabama. He said to Dal, "The young jurisdictional leaders know that you are anointed by the Holy Ghost to preach the Gospel of Jesus Christ and set men, women, boys, and girls free from the bondage of Satan. They know that the fivefold ministry is alive in you. They know that if they allow you to preach, your gifts will make room for you. So, they decided not to allow you to use your spiritual gifts anywhere in the jurisdiction. If you don't use your spiritual gifts, they can't make room for you." Elder Tally further states, "I watched you grow up. I attended school with your older sisters. I will not stand by and allow them to destroy you and your ministry." Dal looked at Elder Tally and said, "I never had any doubt that the vision that was shown me by the Holy Ghost was true. No one can destroy me unless God allows it. My faith and work are totally dependent upon God. He is the one who told me to, "Go into my vineyard and work, and whatever is right, I will pay," my faith is wholly in God!"

Dal continued to fast and pray as he inquired of God about what he should do about the persecution. The Holy Ghost spoke to Dal and said, "Ask Elder Herndon to allow you to use his parking lot for a revival. He will be too ashamed not to allow you to preach in the parking lot." Dal asked pastor Herndon if he could use the church parking lot for an outdoor revival. Pastor Herndon gave his approval with hesitation. The spirit of God moved on the brothers of the church, and they came together and built a platform and a podium for Dal in the parking lot. Dal, as was his custom, fasted and prayed constantly that God through the Holy Ghost would save, heal, deliver, and set free with gifts of the Holy Ghost during the revival. Finally, the day the revival was to begin arrived. About three hours before the revival was to begin, it started to rain very hard. In the south we say, "It's raining cats and dogs." The parking lot was overflowing with water. The grass was saturated with water. The thunder and lightning were threatening, and here was Dal ready to start a revival outside in the adverse weather conditions. The jurisdictional Chairlady of the Evangelist Department was there to help sing and play music for the revival. She played an electric guitar, and because of the weather, she suggested to Dal that they had best move inside the church to get out of the extreme weather conditions. Dal looked at her and said, "God has instructed me to preach outside, and I intend to preach outside tonight if I get wringing wet doing it." Dal and the worshippers sang an opening song and began to pray. While Dal and the worshippers prayed, the Lord sent a strong wind and blew the parking lot dry. The lightening ceased, the thunder stopped rolling, and the sky was without a single cloud. The moon, the stars, and the constellations were clear in the night sky. Praise God for His goodness! When Dal went to the podium to preach, he stated that the Holy Ghost had instructed him to preach on the Holy Ghost every night during the week. Dal preached on the promise of the Holy Ghost from the Old Testament and the Gospels. He preached about the coming of the Holy Ghost from book of the Acts of the Apostles. Dal did not know that there was a wealthy construction owner in attendance who had heard him say that he would speak on the Holy Ghost every night. This brother was there every night because he did not believe there as enough information in the Bible about the Holy Ghost for anyone to preach about it for a whole week. This brother heard the sermons all week on the Holy Ghost, and he accepted the Lord Jesus Christ as his personal savior during the revival. One evening when Dal gave the call to discipleship and prayer, a woman was brought forward who was demon possessed. The demons would turn the woman's body and joints in ways that was unnatural and impossible for humans to do. With authority, he commanded the demons to come out of the woman. All of the demons came out of the woman except the prince of the demons who had possessed her. Dal heard the Holy Ghost say, "This kind is not going out except through fasting and prayer." When Dal heard this, he stopped praying for the woman and asked the congregation to fast the next day until noon specifically for the demon possessed woman. He admonished all of those who promised to fast and pray for the woman not to eat or drink anything until noon on the next day. He said that after fasting and praying, the woman would be delivered from the bondage of Satan. Dal knew from experience that it was of little use to continue praying for the woman until he had obeyed the command of the Holy Ghost. Dal was not aware that the church had been praying for the woman for weeks, but could not cast the demons out of her. Before the worship service ended, the pastor stopped by. Someone told him that Dal had told the people to fast in order for the woman to be set free from Satan. When the pastor was given place to address the congregation before dismissal, he called the woman back and said, "This daughter does not have to wait until tomorrow to be set free from Satan. She is going to be set free tonight." He proceeded to pray for the woman again. The prince of the demons mocked him before the congregation and refused to come out of the woman. The pastor dropped his head in shame and for some unexplainable reason became angry with Dal. The pastor was visibly embarrassed before his congregation. Dal had done nothing wrong. He merely obeyed the command of the Holy Ghost. The next evening when Dal went to the podium, he asked, "How many of you fasted until noon today for this woman's soul?" Those in the congregation who had fasted raised their hands. Dal said, "Before I preach tonight, we are going to loose this woman from the bonds of Satan." As Dal started toward the possessed woman to lay hands on her and pray for her deliverance, the prince of demons came out of the woman. Dal commanded the demon to go back to the pit form which he came. Dal said this because he knew that when demons come out of a person, they are looking for someone to inhabit. Therefore, he ordered the demon back to the pit to ensure that he would not enter into any of the weak worshippers standing around trying to see what was happening. The woman out of whom the demons were cast begin to praise the Lord Jesus with all of her strength. The elderly members of the congregation who had been saved, sanctified, and baptized in the Holy Ghost for forty, fifty, and sixty years began to say, "We've never seen it on this order. We've never seen anything like this before." Dal remembered the first night of the revival when Satan had tried to stop the revival with extreme weather conditions, the rain, the thunder and lightning. He thought about the invitation to go inside because of the weather but, the Holy Ghost had instructed him to preach outside. He remembered the opening prayer of the revival when God sent the wind and blew the parking lot dry. He remembered how after the prayer, there wasn't a cloud in the sky. Instead, the stars, moon, and the constellations could be clearly seen. Dal began to praise and glorify the Lord, "Thank you, Lord. We do receive and enjoy the goodness and blessings from you. Your word is life, and your word gives life. All praises are thine, oh Lord."

On another evening the power of God, the anointing was so great in the service that it seemed as if the heavens were open and all who believed were being healed, delivered, set free, and baptized in the Holy Ghost. A car passed by, backed up, and a woman jumped out of the car and ran into the worship service to the altar. When Dal laid his hands on her, she was instantly slain the in the spirit. She came to herself speaking in tongues and praising God with all that was in her. Later, she testified that she had left Buffalo, New York, several days earlier. She wanted God in her life and didn't know how to go about it or where to find Him. She said she felt empty and just got into her car and started driving, not knowing where she was going or what she would do. She said she wanted God in her life and did not understand how to open up and receive Him. As she testified, she couldn't stop dancing in the spirit and praising God. She shouted, "I've got it! This is what I was looking for! I've got the Holy Ghost!" Dal now understood why God had said preach outside in the parking lot. God had strategically placed him in the parking lot so that this woman from Buffalo, New York, could receive the blessed Holy Ghost. Praise God from whom all blessing flow! After hearing about the success of the outdoor revival, those jurisdictional officials who were persecuting Dal could say nothing except, "Now he's trying to be a wonder." Dal thought to himself, "No. I am not a wonder, but Jesus is the wonder." All things work together for good to those who are in Christ Jesus who are called according to His purpose. Dal didn't quite understand how those who professed to know Jesus Christ could be so against him for simply allowing the anointing of the Holy Ghost and the gifts of God to operate in his life. Dal watched as they destroyed each other and churches in their fight to obtain a position of authority in the church. Church positions were the farthest thing from Dal's mind. He was only interested in doing the will of God to the best of his ability. Those who were persecuting Dal was so blinded by their desire for position and authority that they could not conceive of anyone whose only desire was to please God.

At the Mid-Summer Convocation in 1981, the word had gotten out about how some of the jurisdictional officials were persecuting Dal, so Dal was appointed to two churches, one in Aliceville and the other in Demopolis. The jurisdictional officials wanted it to appear that they were trying to help Dal but, in reality, there was no established church in either Demopolis or Aliceville. Dal pondered the situation and was about to refuse the appointments when the Spirit of the Lord spoke to him and said, "Go there and preach out churches but, you will not be there long." Dal, his wife, Marlyn, and their youngest daughter, Sheila, drove to Aliceville and found an old building that had not been used in quite a long time. In fact, the stray animals had taken up residence in it. Dal and his wife and daughter hosed the inside of the building to get rid of the animal feces. Then they scrubbed the walls and the floor and washed the windows. Then they painted the building inside and out. One of the local churches donated some chairs. Dal went in prayer and asked God to provide him with an organ to provide music for the worship services. Dal had no job except full time evangelism. Dal and one of the young ministers on the Tuscaloosa District went to a music store to get an organ but, had no money. Dal asked the young minister if he could believe with him that God would touch the heart of the owner of the music store so that he would give us an organ. Dal cautioned the young minister not to accompany him into the store if he did not have faith to believe with him. The two of them went into the store and Dal asked to speak to the owner. When the owner came out, Dal greeted him in the name of the Lord. He told the owner that he was starting a church in Aliceville, and he needed an organ for the choir. Dal told the owner that he had no eight to five job and therefore, couldn't promise to pay him anything. The owner looked at Dal intently. Dal reiterated, "The Lord needs an organ." The owner spoke and said, "I have a large organ here that my wife used to teach music lessons. It's in excellent condition. My wife just wanted a new organ." He asked Dal if he could have someone at the church about 5:00 p.m. to unload the organ. He said that his workers got off in an hour and would not be able to unload the organ. He said that he would have them load the organ onto the delivery truck before they got off, but would need someone at the church to unload it. Dal told him that he would be at the Aliceville church at five o'clock with someone to unload the organ. The music store owner arrived at the Aliceville church at five o'clock with a large, top of the line Wurlitzer organ. Dal and those with him began to thank the music store owner for the organ. After unloading the organ, they began to praise the Lord for His goodness. Dal said, "My God, we do receive and enjoy the goodness and blessing of you." Dal took one look at the countenance of the young minister who had accompanied him to the store and had helped unload the organ and knew that this experience had increased his faith in God exponentially. It would be this young minister who would eventually pastor the church in Demopolis that Dal would establish there. Dal found several families in Aliceville who wanted to have a Pentecostal-Holiness church there. So, they organized and began having worship services. Dal even persuaded one Muslim family to give up Islam and accept Jesus as their personal savior. Dal explained to them that Muslims, Christians, and Jews worship the same God. He explained that both Ismael and Isaac grew up in Abraham's house. He took the Koran and showed them where the Prophet Mohammad spoke of the coming Messiah. Then he explained that Jesus was the promised Messiah. The entire family accepted Jesus as their personal savior and joined the Aliceville church.

When Dal arrived in Demopolis, the small church where he used to preach every year during his South-Central Alabama evangelistic tour had been auctioned off for taxes. Dal understood that the state did not tax churches. He decided to locate a lawyer to help recover the church property. While on his way to the lawyer's office, the Holy Ghost spoke and said, "Don't hire a lawyer. Locate the person who bought the property at the auction and go talk with him." Dal obeyed the Holy Spirit. When Dal met Mr. Smith who had purchased the property with the highest bid at the auction, Mr. Smith began to explain to Dal why he had bid on the property. He explained that his mother had worked with the church until the founding pastor died. The presiding Bishop had appointed various pastors to the church, but none of them stayed for very long. So, the church had just sat there and eventually fell down with no one to make repairs. Dal went to see the building. It was literally laying on its side. The building was uninhabitable, but the land was there on which to build another church. Mr. Smith told Dal about the many charlatans who had claimed the property but, could not produce credentials to prove that they were authorized by the Church of God in Christ to handle the property. Dal opened his briefcase and took out his appointment papers for Mr. Smith the see. Furthermore, Dal told Mr. Smith that he knew his mother from the years when he had conducted revivals there. Mr. Smith said, "Let's go see my mother. If she says that you are legitimate, you can have the property for the one hundred seven dollars I paid at auction. My mother worked so hard with the former pastor that I did not want to see anyone get the property except the rightful owners. When Mr. Smith's mother saw Dal, she ran to him and gave him a big hug. She told her son, "This is the evangelist who used to preach here in revival every year." Mr. Smith turned to Dal and said, "The church property is yours. I also own a construction company. When you get ready to build, I will build the church building for you." Dal rejoiced and began to praise God for

His goodness. After Dal recovered the church property and held services under a tent for about a year, the Holy Spirit spoke and said, "Dal, your time here is over. You must preach the Gospel of Jesus Christ in other places also." Dal called the presiding jurisdictional Bishop and ask him to send a pastor for the flock at the Demopolis church.

Dal's next revival was in Enterprise, Alabama, where Elder James T. Hollister was the pastor. While in revival at the Enterprise Church of God in Christ, Dal met a young minister who was in the military. He was stationed at Fort Rucker near Ozark, Al. The young minister had made a mistake in his life. He had gotten a child out of wedlock by a young woman who was a member of the Wayside C.O.G.I.C. Dal perceived that the young man was godly sorrowful about what he had done but, the church would not forgive him. He talked to Dal about his situation while Dal was conducting a revival in Enterprise. Dal instructed the young minister to go before the church and confess openly because he had brought an open shame on the church. The young man did as Dal had instructed him. The church forgave him, and the Lord forgave him. He began to praise and magnify the Lord with all of his strength. The young minister asked Dal if he would come to Fort Rucker and conduct a revival on the base at the fort's chapel. Dal told him to arrange for the revival and he would be there to preach. In the meantime, Dal had begun a job as an industrial engineer technician for Jim Walter Resources Division of mining. To get to Fort Rucker in time to preach, Dal had to average at least seventy miles per hour but, the maximum speed limit was only fifty-five miles per hour. The second night of the revival, Dal was stopped by the highway patrol officer for speeding. Dal explained to the officer why he was speeding. He told the officer about the revival at Fort Rucker. The officer went to his car and called on the phone. Dal did not know who or why he called, but when the officer came back to Dal's car he said, "Reverend, for the duration of this revival, you can average seventy miles per hour every night and no one will stop you for speeding. Do not go faster than seventy miles per hour." Every night when the anointing would begin to heal, deliver, and set people free, a young woman would get up as if she was praising God, but her spirit was demonic. Dal recognized that the woman was possessed by demons, but he did not cast them out. On the way back home, Dal's wife, Marlyn, asked, "When are you going to do something about the woman? She is demon possessed." Dal acknowledged to Marlyn that she was correct in her assessment of the woman, but the Holy Ghost had not allowed him to cast the demons out yet. Dal explained to his wife that when the woman gets up and disturbs the worship services, she was asking for help in the only way the demons allowed her to do so. Since the demons were in control of her mind and body, it was her way of asking for help. The next night the Holy Ghost spoke to Dal and said, "Set the woman free." When Dal laid his hands on the woman and began to rebuke Satan, commanding the demons to come out of the woman, the demons caused the woman to fall to the floor trying to get away from the anointing that was upon Dal. Dal went down to the floor with her and kept on praying, commanding the demons to come out of the woman. The woman's body began to move like a serpent across the floor trying to get away from the anointing of God. Dal appointed four men to hold the woman still while he prayed for her. With four men holding the woman down, as Dal continued to pray for her, the demons caused the woman's body to levitate in the air. Then the woman screamed with the most spine-tingling scream Dal had ever heard in his life as the demons released her and took flight. He body floated back down to the floor, and she got up speaking in tongues and praising God for His goodness. Instead of being full of demons, this woman was now full of the Holy Ghost. The Sargent-Major, who was present every night, asked Dal, "Is this real? Is this really happening? Does it take all of this?" Dal responded, "It takes all of this and more." Dal praised God and said, "We do receive and enjoy the blessing and goodness of you, Lord Jesus, the will of the Father, the amen of glory, the hallelujah of heaven. To God be the glory through His Son, Jesus the Christ."

While living in Cleveland, OH, Dal had attended Cuyahoga Community College and Cleveland State University to find answers to some fundamental questions regarding the major world religions. Dal did not have doubts concerning his God in his life as a way of life. He wanted to know the origins of the world's major religions and how they evolved into their present forms. He wanted to understand the origins of the various Christian denominations and why there was so much disagreement over the interpretation of scripture. Dal wanted to comprehend how Christians, Muslims, and Jews could all look forward to a promised Messiah and yet disagree vehemently concerning the Messiahship of Jesus the Christ. He wanted to justify the Bible historically as well as religiously. Dal's purpose was to prepare himself to understand all of the world's religions in order to be better prepared to convince all people that Jesus, the only begotten Son of God, truly is the promised deliverer and the only one who can save mankind from sin. Dal studied religious studies as well as religious philosophy. He read book after book after book written by the great writers and thinkers from ancient to modern times. He studied religious and non-religious philosophers. Dal sought out the difference between theologians and philosophers since both claimed to seek the absolute truth. Dal asked, "How can anyone embrace a scriptural interpretation that contradicted several other scriptures?" After much research and study, and the guiding of the Holy Ghost, Dal came to the conclusion that, the Bible never contradicts itself, but rather that people use it in ways that it was not intended to be used. Anytime a person interprets a Biblical scripture in such a way as to contradict another scripture, that person's interpretation is erroneous. The Bible does not contradict itself! Rather it complements and supplements itself. The Bible can only be understood from a participant's viewpoint. The living word of God must be in you, and you must be in the word of God if you want to fully comprehend it. You must first have the Holy Ghost abiding in you, then, ask God for the wisdom that comes from above. Jesus said it best in the Gospel of St. John, "But when He, the Spirit of truth comes, He will guide you into all truth." Again, Jesus said, "I will ask the Father, and He will give you another Helper, that He may be with you forever; that is the Spirit of Truth, who the world cannot receive, because it does not behold Him or know Him because He abides with you and will be in you." Only those in whom the Holy Ghost dwells has the ability to fully comprehend God's living word. Those in the world cannot receive this wisdom, indeed, they cannot see it. It is spiritually discerned. After a year of college, Dal received an invitation to conduct a revival in Waterloo, Iowa. He had run track for Cuyahoga Community College's track team and had been given a scholarship for the following year. Dal gave that up to obey the call of God. He went to Iowa and preached for two weeks there. God, through Jesus Christ, manifested himself there with signs and wonders, and mighty acts, and gifts of the Holy Ghost. One night, Dal preached "Teach Us to say yes." After the sermon, instead of making the call to discipleship, Dal told the worshippers that, "There will be no prayer lines or tarrying services tonight." He said, "The Holy Ghost says victory comes on the wings of praise. So, whatever you believe God for, begin to praise Him for it." The worshippers began to praise God with all their hearts, souls, and strength. Suddenly, a sound like a rushing mighty wind came into the sanctuary and worshippers were slain in the spirit all over the sanctuary. There was no room to walk in the aisles without having to step over someone slain in the spirit. Worshippers were speaking in other tongues as the spirit gave the utterance. People were healed, delivered, and set free from whatever their bondage had been. African Americans, Caucasians, hippies, yippies, educators, and all who dared to obey Dal's directive to praise God, found themselves overcome by the power of the Holy Ghost. Professors from the University of Northern Iowa were asking, "Does it really take all of this?" Dal answered in the affirmative, "This and more." The glory of God filled the place. When Dal left Iowa at the end of two weeks, the church was filled beyond capacity and the altar was overflowing with people seeking the indwelling presence of the Holy Ghost. Dal boarded a train and returned to Ohio, but as soon as he arrived home, his wife told him that the pastor from Iowa had called and said that people were asking for him to return to Waterloo to continue the revival. The pastor said that he could not handle the people and was asking Dal to return to Iowa immediately. Dal's wife washed his clothes and prepared Dal for his return to Iowa. Upon Dal's return to Waterloo, Iowa, the Holy Ghost continued to glorify Jesus Christ with signs and wonders and might acts in the Holy Ghost. Dal didn't know it at the time, but he would eventually spend nine months in Iowa.

While Dal resided in Cleveland, Ohio, he met a young Elder who wanted to become an evangelist. So, when Dal left for the revival in Iowa, he allowed the young Elder to accompany him on the trip to Iowa. During the first two weeks, the young Elder proved to be a real asset to Dal and his ministry. Upon their return to Iowa, the aged pastor became jealous and started devising ways to get the people to follow him instead of Jesus. There were two nuns from the local convent who had attended the revival services. One evening, Dal allowed them to sing during the services. The nuns were young and attractive. Usually, after revival services Dal and the young Elder would return to the parsonage, have a cup of hot tea and a bowl of soup, then retire for the night. The routine changed when the aged pastor and the young Elder began visiting the nuns after services each night. They would leave Dal at the parsonage each night after services and visit with the nuns who were supposed to be in the convent by a certain time. Dal knew that the aged pastor was trying to get the young Elder to sin so that he would lose his anointing in the Holy Ghost. So, Dal took the young elder aside and talked to him about the importance of being always ready to do service for God. This included living a sanctified and holy life so the Holy Ghost could use him at any time. Dal admonished the young Elder to continue to live a life worthy of the vocation of preaching the Gospel of Jesus the Christ. He reminded him that when one is doing evangelism, be always aware of Satan's devices and in all places because Satan will rise up anywhere at any time to try to impede the salvation of souls. Dal told the young Elder that Satan tempts one to sin in order to separate one from his/her source of power. The Holy Ghost indwells one in order to empower one to do the work of salvation. Without the Holy Ghost, one has no anointing or power with which to operate in Jesus Christ's vineyard. Dal warned the young Elder, "If Satan succeeds in separating you from your source of power (the Holy Ghost) by getting you to yield to temptation, then you have no authority to cast him out of those who come to the altar for help. Your body is the temple of the Holy Ghost. If you defile the body through sin, the Holy Ghost can no longer dwell there because he does not dwell in unclean temples." Dal's fervent warnings were to no avail. The young Elder kept on going out with the aged pastor to see the young, attractive nuns.The priest asked them about their visits to the convent and ask that they stop but, the nuns   would let them in secretly. Finally, after several nights out with the aged pastor and the nuns, the young Elder's anointing left him. During revival services, the young Elder continued to go through the motions pretending that he was still under the anointing of the Holy Ghost but, Dal knew that his anointing had left him. Dal called the young elder aside and informed him that he was sending him back home to Cleveland because it too dangerous to war against Satan without the full anointing of the Holy Ghost. Dal would spend the next seven months in Waterloo, Iowa, fighting familiar spirits and outright witchcraft.

The church leaders allowed Dal to live at the parsonage with the aged pastor for the next several months. Many of them asked Dal to stay and take over the pastorate of the church because they wanted to get rid of the aged pastor who they believed was practicing witchcraft. Dal told them that he had never undermined anyone in ministry, and he would not do so now. When Dal became aware that the pastor was involved in witchcraft, he prepared to return to Cleveland, but the people wanted him to stay and the Holy Ghost said, "Stay until I tell you to leave." The Holy Ghost kept Dal in Waterloo, Iowa, for several months teaching him how people work with familiar spirits and witchcraft to harm those who are unaware and not fasting and praying as they ought to be for the salvation of their souls and the souls of others. The aged pastor went to the church leaders and requested that they put Dal out of the parsonage, but the church leaders refused and instead told the aged pastor that he was free to leave but Dal, could stay there as long as he wanted to stay. This caused the aged pastor to attempt to use witchcraft on Dal. Dal always drank milk for breakfast and dinner. So, he kept cartons of milk in the refrigerator. One morning Dal opened a carton of milk and poured out one glass for breakfast, but when he returned to the parsonage in the late afternoon, the carton was empty except for about six ounces. This puzzled Dal since the aged pastor had told him when he first arrived in Iowa, that he did not drink milk. There was no one else in the parsonage except Dal and the aged pastor. So, why was there only six ounces of milk left in the carton? While Dal thought on this, the Holy Ghost spoke to him and said, "Do not drink it. Let it stay there until I tell you what to do." Dal obeyed and opened another carton of milk. When Dal left the parsonage the next day and returned in the afternoon, the carton of milk was empty again except for about six ounces of milk. Dal remembered what the Holy Ghost had said to him the day before. "Don't drink it. Let it stay there until I tell you what to do." Dal opened another carton of milk for dinner. This continued for about eight days. Finally, the Holy Ghost spoke and said, "Take the milk from the almost empty cartons and make a glassful, but don't drink it. Pour it down the sink." Dal did this for four days until the milk from the empty cartons was gone. Dal did not drink it but, poured it down the sink in obedience to the Holy Ghost. The aged pastor thought that Dal had drank the milk left in the cartons. So, he would sit and watch Dal as if he expected something to happen to him. After approximately a week, the pastor's look of expectation turned to a look of awe and wonder. He couldn't figure out why, whatever it was that he was trying to get into Dal's body was not working. Next, the aged pastor attempted to put something out through the heating system. Every night at about eleven o'clock, he would leave the parsonage and return just before midnight and go straight to the basement where the furnace was located. The furnace would have been loaded with coal before he left the parsonage, so there was no reason for him to put anything in the furnace until the next day. Every night at midnight the aged pastor would go to the basement and the coal burning furnace and put something in it. Then he would come back upstairs and turn the thermostat up as high as it would go. Afterward, he would sit in the corner of the living room and watch Dal as if he expected something to happen to him. One day, as Dal passed by one of the heating vents, the force coming from the vent almost knocked Dal off his feet. The demonic powers of darkness were so great that Dal could feel their presence everywhere in the place. Dal wanted to leave and was ready to leave but, the Holy Ghost said, "Stay. Not a hair of your head will be harmed." Again, Dal stayed on in obedience to the will of God. Dal prayed and fasted continually, knowing that he was not fighting against flesh and blood, but against principalities, spiritual wickedness in high places, and against the rulers of the darkness of this world.

One day, as Dal lay on his bed meditating and praying, he felt an evil presence pass over him. Dal kept on praying in the spirit. When Dal felt the evil presence pass over him the second time, he realized what was about to happen. He had been there before. As Dal started to call the name of Jesus and at the same time turn from his back to his side to get to his feet, the demonic forces attacked him. Dal lay there on his back struggling against an invisible demonic power with all his physical strength, with all of his heart, and with all of his mind. Dal could not say a word. He could not move a muscle though he was using all of his physical, mental, and spiritual strength. Dal had but one thing that was not bound, his mind. He still controlled his mind. Dal's mind was fixed on Jesus when the demonic forces attacked him. Dal lay there thinking, "Though I can't say a word or move a muscle, my mind is fixed on Jesus. And I'm going to think Jesus with such conviction and force that Satan will have to release me." Dal's tongue was fixed to say Jesus and his body was pushing against Satan as he was trying to get off his back when Satan attacked him. With his mind fixed on Jesus, Dal resisted Stan with all his might. When Satan released Dal, it was like someone pushing against a door with all their strength, but someone on the opposite side is preventing the door from opening and then suddenly releases the door. When Satan took flight from struggling with Dal, Dal's body rose two feet off the bed as he flipped over onto his side. His head snapped around, and the name "Jesus" screamed from his mouth. Dal got up and went throughout the parsonage rebuking every foul, demonic spirit from hell. When Dal opened the door to the aged pastor's bedroom as he rebuked the evil forces, he noticed that he had one sheet on his bed and the heating vents in his bedroom had been disconnected from the furnace. Walking into his bedroom was like walking into a deep freeze. Immediately, the Holy Ghost spoke to Dal and said, "It is finished. You have seen the things I wanted you to see. Go and preach the Gospel of Jesus Christ everywhere. I will be with you always. Nothing shall harm you. You are free to return to Cleveland." On the way back to Cleveland, the Holy Ghost gave Dal a new sermon, "Know Your Enemy." It is not the evil man, woman, boy, or girl who is our enemy, but rather Satan, the Prince of Darkness who can indwell persons just as the Holy Ghost can indwell persons. There is no middle ground in this war against the forces of evil. Either the Holy Spirit indwells you or the forces of evil indwells you. Neither of them can enter your heart unless you invite them in. It's your choice!!!!!!!

When Dal left Cleveland, Ohio, nine months earlier to preach Jesus Christ in Waterloo, Iowa, he had given up a scholarship in track in obedience to the Holy Ghost. Upon his return to Cleveland, he was offered an academic scholarship as well as a track scholarship. Dal now understands from experience that whatever one gives up for the sake of the Gospel of Jesus Christ, God always gives back more than one gave up. Dal witnesses this truth everywhere he preaches the Gospel of Jesus Christ.

In December 1981, Dal was called to Cleveland, to conduct a revival during Christmas. Dal had only enough money for gasoline one way, but he believed that God through the Holy Ghost was leading him to Cleveland to preach to the congregation at Victory Temple C.O.G.I.C. It had been a while since Dal had lived in Cleveland. He and his family had moved to Birmingham, Alabama. Some of the C.O.G.I.C. Elders in Cleveland had been unfaithful to their spouses, and Dal had the misfortune of bumping into several of them with their girlfriends in several places such as the Greyhound Bus Station and other places in Cleveland. Some of the guilty preachers started rumors about Dal in order to cover their own ungodly behaviors. They had reported that Dal had divorced his wife and was living with another woman. This was done maliciously because Dal had innocently walked up on them in compromising situations. Dal had never said anything to anyone else about these ministers' adulterous behavior but, they maliciously attacked Dal's reputation to cover their own ungodly deeds. Dal had been taught to allow the deeds of evil done in secret to remain in secret so that some innocent soul with confidence in that particular person would not be destroyed. So, Dal had never told anyone about these Elders' infidelity to their spouses. After the pastor at Victory Temple C.O.G.I.C. heard Dal preach the first night of the revival, he said to Dal, "I now understand why certain ministers don't like you." Dal asked, "What do you mean?" The pastor said, "You are preaching the unadulterated Gospel of Jesus Christ. Don't you know that no one is preaching that anymore?" Dal responded, "Isn't that what Jesus anointed us to preach? Woe unto me if I preach not the Gospel of Jesus Christ." The pastor continued, "You are hated and persecuted because you dare to preach the unadulterated Gospel of Christ. Keep on preaching it. Someone has to preach it if people are going to be saved from their sins."

The second night of the revival, Dal's sermon asked the question, "Is There No Balm in Gilead?" As Dal exorcized demons from a young man during prayer, some of the demons came out and attacked some of the other worshippers who were standing in close proximity trying to see the exorcism. Dal had to leave the young man momentarily to pray for those being attacked by the demons. Some of them were physically being choked by the demons. Dal prayed until the demons released those being attacked, then continued casting the demons out of the young man. On another evening, as the worshippers were being blessed with salvation and gifts of the Holy Ghost, a demon possessed man walked into the sanctuary and proceeded to undress. Dal was preaching, "Lord, Teach Us to Say Yes." While Dal preached, the man took off his shoes, his shirt, his belt, and then started to take off his jeans. That's when Dal stopped preaching and walked to the back of the sanctuary where the man was undressing and began commanding the demons to come out of the man in the Name of Jesus Christ. All the demons came out of the man except the prince of darkness who was over them. The prince of demons spoke to Dal and named all of the heavenly constellations and said that he had traveled through all of them. Dal said, "I know. You came through them when you were cast out of heaven into the earth. Now hold your peace and come out of the man." The demon started speaking with other tongues. Dal, who had the gift of tongues and the interpretation of tongues, began to speak to the demon in tongues, saying the same thing that he was saying in English, "Come out of the man in the Name of Jesus Christ." As Dal motioned for some of the brethren to come to the back of the church to hold the man while he prayed for him, the demon ran quickly out of the sanctuary into the street leaving his shoes, shirt, and belt behind. Dal and the brethren ran out behind the man, but he seemed to vanish into thin air. There was no sign of the man anywhere. He was nowhere to be found. Dal never saw the man again. He believed that it was Satan in the form of a man who entered the sanctuary that night. The revival was everything that Dal had prayed for. People were healed of various diseases, demons were cast out of many, many were saved, sanctified, and baptized in the Holy Ghost and Fire. Backsliders were reclaimed and filled with the Holy Ghost.

Dal had expected God to work wonders in Cleveland because Satan had tried to prevent him from getting there. On the way to Cleveland, about four o'clock in the morning as Dal approached Nashville, Tennessee, the alternator on his car stopped working. There was no garage opened where Dal could get the alternator repaired. Dal stopped at a service station and the attendant told him that he might find a place in Louisville, Kentucky, where he could get the alternator repaired if the battery held up that long. Dal could have tried to go back to Birmingham, Alabama, since it was roughly the same distance from Nashville as Louisville, Kentucky. God wanted Dal in Cleveland, Ohio, so Dal left Nashville heading for Cleveland. As Dal approached Louisville, the Holy Ghost spoke and said, "Don't stop in Louisville, keep driving." Marlyn, Dal's wife was in the passenger seat half asleep when Dal told her what the Holy Ghost had said. She told him to do what the Holy Ghost said. Dal drove all day, from dawn to dark with the alternator light coming on and going off, recharging the battery every twenty minutes. As darkness descended upon them, Dal turned on the headlights and the car stopped running. A few minutes later, an Ohio State Trooper arrived and told Dal that he knew a mechanic about thirty miles off the interstate who would tow us to his garage and repair the alternator, but that he would charge us a high price. Dal said, "Call him." Dal had about forty dollars total. He didn't know what would happen, but he believed that God would provide a way for him to get to Cleveland. Dal called his wife's parents and told them where they were, just south of Mansfield, Ohio, approximately eighty miles out of Cleveland. About an hour later, the mechanic arrived and towed Dal's car to his garage. He invited Dal and his wife and daughter into his home and his spouse gave them food and drink while he repaired the alternator. When he had finished, he looked at Dal and said, "I am not going to charge you anything for the labor. If you can pay me for the parts I used, that will be fine. Dal said, "I have forty dollars total." The mechanic said, "Consider the whole thing a Christmas present. You don't owe me anything." As Dal prepared to leave the mechanics home, he prayed a very special blessing upon his home and his business. As Dal continued his journey to Cleveland, he knew that the mechanic, his family, and his business was indeed blessed. Also, Dal had again witnessed the gracious providence of God when one is obedient to his command. Dal had no money to pay the mechanic for his services but, he had the power of God unto salvation. Dal told the mechanic in the words of Peter and John in the third chapter of the book of Acts, "Silver and gold have I none, but such as I have, I give to you. In the name of Jesus Christ, be blessed."

After completing the revival, Dal returned to Alabama. During the Official day of the Holy Convocation, Dal and the jurisdictional Elders were in Sunday School class when one of the Elders asked a question that had absolutely nothing to do with the Sunday School lesson. The question was, "If something sinful is going on in the local church, who does God/the Holy Ghost reveal it to?" Dal knew that the question was a loaded one. He was puzzled as to why that question was asked since it had nothing to do with the lesson. When Dal looked at the expression on the face of the Elder who had asked the questions, he could see that the elder thought he knew the answer already and was merely seeking reinforcement from the jurisdictional pastors in attendance. And just as the Elder asking the question expected, most of the pastors stood one by one and affirmed that God would only reveal things wrong in the local church to the pastor. This pleased the pastor who had asked the question and reinforced the conclusion that he had already drawn. Dal had heard this same question time and again in various other jurisdictions and the answer was always the same, namely, God only reveals to the pastor sins being committed in the local church. Dal had heard this question-and-answer scenario time and time again. Only this time, the Holy Ghost had given Dal the gift of wisdom and had commissioned him to "Teach the Word and don't hold back. Fear not." So, Dal felt compelled to let the pastors know that they were in error according to scripture. Dal was recognized by the teacher and stood to give his input on the question. He opened his Bible to I Corinthian 12:28 and Ephesians 4: 11-12 and read to the pastors and elders the list of offices that God had put in the church, specifically, for the up building and edification of the church. Dal said to the Elders, with much respect and honor, that Jesus had placed more than the pastor in the church to strengthen the body of Christ. He reminded them that Jesus had placed apostles, prophets, evangelists, pastors, and teachers in the church to edify the church. Dal stated that God would reveal to anyone who is fully empowered by the Holy Ghost when sin is in the local church. He/she may not have the authority the change the situation, but they can certainly pray for deliverance.

Many of the pastors disagreed with Dal's answer in spite of the supporting scriptures he read to them. Scriptures that clearly supported Dal's conclusion without contradicting other scripture. After Sunday School, Dal watched as pastors and jurisdictional officials told the bishop what Dal had said in Sunday School. They gave him the scriptures that Dal had read and requested that he correct Dal when he got up for his official address. Dal watched all of this in planning. So, after Sunday School had been dismissed and everyone was preparing for the official procession, Dal decided to leave for home rather than be preached on in front of the entire convocation. He thought to himself, "I'm not staying to be preached on today because of my spiritual gifts." As Dal left the convention center walking toward the parking lot where his car was parked, a still small voice spoke to him and said, "go back in there and march in the procession. I will reveal myself again to you today." Dal went back inside and took part in the processional. Since there were not enough seats on the platform for all the Elders, Dal and many of the Elders were seated on the front row directly in front of the podium from which the bishop would give his Official Address. As if providence had provided it, Dal's seat was right in front of the podium. The only way the bishop could not see Dal would be to close his eyes and refuse to see. When the Bishop started his address, Dal was looking directly up into his face. The bishop had one of the pastors read the same scriptures that Dal had citied during Sunday School. He struggled to find a way to interpret them in a way that would support what the pastors had concluded during Sunday School, namely, that the Holy Ghost reveals sin or wrongdoing in the local church to the pastor only. Dal watched as the bishop struggled, and struggled, and struggled trying to say what the pastors wanted him to say. He tried three times, and each time the Holy Ghost over-shadowed him, and he said the same thing that Dal had said during Sunday School. After the third attempt, the bishop turned to the pastors and officials seated behind him and said in an apologetic tone, "Brothers, this is not Bishop. This is the book (meaning the Bible)." Through all of this and much, much more, Jesus has always let Dal know that he belonged to Him and that He was ever present to deliver him from whatever or whoever Satan uses to hinder the work of the Holy Ghost.

Dal is always prayerful that he will be able to endure the things that Satan brings against him because of the Gospel of Jesus Christ. He knows that he must hold out until the end in order to be ready when Jesus comes again. He praises God for the many times that he has sustained him and revealed Himself to him in many ways and at various times and places in his ministry. Dal is thankful when he remembers all the tests and trials that have made him steadfast in his growth from grace to grace and from faith to faith. He remembers earlier in his ministry when his slacks were worn, and he had no money to buy new ones. He remembers those slacks that had been patched and worn so thin that one could literally hold them up and see through them. Dal remembers how after he had been blessed with a new set of clothes, God revealed to him that there was nothing to hold the slacks together except the Holy Ghost. He remembers simply holding those slacks up and watching them just completely fall apart in front of his eyes and then hearing the Lord say, "It was Me holding those pants together until I blessed you with more clothes. Dal remembers being hit by a truck while moving from Cleveland, Ohio, to Birmingham, Alabama; how God preserved him, his wife, and daughter from injury and harm. The U- Haul truck Dal was driving cartwheeled four hundred sixty feet and landed on the gas tank side but didn't explode. None of the family spent time in the hospital. Dal remembers living in Massachusetts and preaching the gospel of Jesus Christ there. New England is heavily Catholic territory. While there, Dal noticed the widespread use of the cross symbol on the churches, both Catholic and Protestant. Dal noticed in large Catholic churches, that there was always a cross with a European on it located in the very prominent place. When the worshippers enter the sanctuary the first thing they did was fall on their knees in obeisance to the image and make a cross symbol across their bodies. One day as Dal passed by one of the old historic cemeteries, he noticed that a lot of the gravestones displayed the cross symbol engraved on them while others were cut in the shape of a cross. Others had various other Catholic symbols attached to them. As Dal pondered these things, something he had been seeking for a long time became clearer. The image of the beast spoken of in the Book of Revelation, chapter 13, is the cross symbol. Christians all over the world represent their religion with the cross symbol. Most meeting places have the cross symbol located on them in extremely conspicuous locations. Dal had several questions that he wanted answered regarding Christianity: is the Bible really the infallible written word of God and has it been tempered with? Jesus and Christianity developed in the east and spread to the west. Where did the west get something so new and different that they now have to evangelize the east? If the abomination of desolation spoken of by Daniel took place in the Maccabean era as taught by Christian theology, why does Jesus' apostles expect it to happen in their lifetime? What is the abomination of desolation? Regarding the "great persecution;" is it yet to come as Christian theology teaches, or is it already in progress (the 4th beast versus the Saints of most high)? If those who receive the mark of the beast in their forehead or right hand, or worship the beast and his image will be cast into the Lake of Fire, don't we need to identify the beast, his number, his mark, his image, and his name? So, what man does the number 666 refer? What city represents Babylon, the great? How does one, "come out of Babylon?" Why is the cross symbol so prevalent among Christians? Is Jesus returning to redeem Christians or his Saints?

THE REVELATION

While Dal pondered these questions, he was instructed by the Holy Ghost to do a comparative study of Daniel and Revelation. Dal spent about three years listening to the Holy Ghost give insight into the present world system and how it came to be. It is in this light that the remainder of this book will identify, define, and explain how the "world system" works and how it has replaced the faith that was once delivered to the Saints (Jude 1:3). We will look closely at the Book of Daniel and Revelation while including other scriptures that affirm what Daniel and John refers to in their writings. My hope is that this book will cause many to reassess the foundation upon which they find themselves standing. We will bring history and scripture together to show/demonstrate how western Christianity has replaced the early church (Jesus' first apostles) with a false church which has become the present "world system" that is ruling globally. The second chapter in the Book of Daniel identifies that last five earthly kingdoms beginning from Babylon to the ancient of days (God.) King Nebuchadnezzar of Babylon had a dream concerning the last five early kingdoms, but he could not remember the dream. After seeking advice from his wise men, astrologers, and counselors, he found no one who could tell him his dream. So, Nebuchadnezzar gave a decree to destroy all the wise men of Babylon. When Arioch, the captain of the king's guard came to Daniel to kill him, Daniel persuaded Arioch to petition the king for more time to allow Daniel and his companions to go before the "God of Heaven" concerning this secret vision so that Daniel, Hananiah, Michael, and Azariah would not be killed with the rest of the wise men of Babylon. After Daniel and his companions sought God in prayer, Nebuchadnezzar's vision was revealed to Daniel in a night vision. Appropriately, the first thing Daniel and his companions did following the revelation was praise the "God of Heaven" for His wisdom and might and for making the king's vision known to them. Next, they used this moment as an opportunity to testify to the king about the "God of Heaven," who reveals secrets and makes known what shall be in the future. Notice that Daniel does not take credit for the revelation but gives God all the credit (glory). Daniel chapter 2, verse 31-35 describes the image that was the centerpiece of the king's vision. The image's head was gold, his breast and arms were silver, his belly and thighs were brass, his legs were iron, and his feet were iron and part clay. Lastly, a stone was cut out without hands which breaks the image into pieces small enough to be carried away by the summer wind. The stone cut out with hands, became a great mountain that fills the entire earth. This was the dream; the interpretation is yet to come.

Daniel chapter 2, verses 36-45 gives the interpretation of the king's dream. The image represented the last four earthly kingdoms. The head of gold was Babylon. The breasts and arms of silver represents the Medes and Persians (particularly the Persians). The belly and thighs of brass represents Greece and Alexander the great. The legs of iron with feet part iron and part clay represents the Roman Empire and the Catholic Church. The stone cut out without hands is (God) who reclaimed the entire earth. The Kingdom of God is an everlasting Kingdom which shall never be destroyed.

Let us look at the 4th Kingdom, which is identified with the Roman Empire, which morphed into the Catholic Church to ensure the survival of the holy Roman Empire. Daniel Chapter 2, verse 40, the Kingdom (empire) is as strong as iron; breaks into pieces and subdues all things; breaks in pieces and bruises; is divided but has in it the strength of iron. The toes of the feet were part iron and part clay meaning the Kingdom will be partly strong and partly broken. The iron in the toes represent the Catholic churches, while the clay represents the Protestant churches. The Catholic Church is strong because it is based on one false theology which is its foundation. The Protestants are broken because all of them have differing doctrines. However, they are all buttressed by the doctrine/theology inherited from the Catholic Church. Hence, the 4th Kingdom is the (holy Roman Empire/Catholic Church/western Christianity) is partly strong and partly broken. The extended meaning of the iron mixed with miry clay shows that the Catholic and Protestants shall not cleave one to another just as clay and iron does not mix. The (Christians/Catholics) shall mingle themselves with the seed of men (Jesus), but they shall not cleave/bond one to another. Here is the Catholic Church attempting to replace the true Church of Jesus (the seed) after years of persecuting the church (the true Church of Jesus) which was founded upon the foundation of the apostles and prophets with Jesus, the Messiah, being the chief cornerstone (Ephesians 2:19-20). Daniel saw this false church/false salvation which would attempt to replace the true Church of Jesus, the Messiah. This is what Daniel meant when he says, "mingle with the seed of men," (Jesus) "but they will not cleave one to another even as iron is not mixed with clay." Later, you will see that this false church replacing the true church is what Daniel refers to as the "abomination that makes desolate" or "the taking away of the daily sacrifice." This 4th kingdom is the one in charge of the world government in the time epoch that Jesus calls "this generation" and his true apostles called "the last days." This is the period in which we live today (in the era of the preaching of the everlasting gospel of Jesus, the Messiah). This world system will not be destroyed until the Heavenly Father, (stone cut out without hands) "the ancient of days" reclaims his earthly kingdom and gives it to the Saints. This will be the 5th and everlasting Kingdom upon the earth. The 7th and 8th chapters of Daniel throw more light and understanding upon the things that have been discussed up to this point. Daniel, Chapter 7, verses 7-27 describe the 4th beast (Kingdom on earth) Roman Empire. This 4th Kingdom is dreadful, terrible, exceedingly strong with great iron teeth. It "devoured and break in pieces and stomps the residue with his feet." It was different from all the earthly kingdoms that had appeared on earth previously. Furthermore, it had ten horns; three of which were, "Plucked up by the roots," "by another little horn that had eyes like the eyes of a man and a mouth speaking great things." Verses 7-14 paints a picture of the God of heaven taking/redeeming his earth from the 4th kingdom and giving it to the "son of man." Whose Kingdom, Dominion, and Glory shall never be destroyed. Next, Daniel is given the interpretation of the vision by an Angel. Again, the 4 earthly kingdoms are identified from Daniel Chapter two (2). The 5th Kingdom (the Kingdom of God) destroys all the earthly kingdoms and institutes the heavenly Father's everlasting Kingdom under the leadership of his only begotten son, Jesus, the son of man. He and His Saints possesses the Kingdom forever and ever. Daniel then asks the Angel specifically about the 4th beast which was different from all other beasts. The beast that made war with the Saints and prevailed against them until the "ancient of days," came and took the Kingdom and gave it to Jesus (the son of man) and to the Saints. The description of the fourth beast/4th Kingdom is identical to that given in Daniel, chapter two, except for the introduction of the ten horns and the little horn that replaces three of the ten. Verse 25 of chapter seven shows, again the attack on the Saints of the highest and the beast against them as shown in chapter two. This is affirmation of the attempt of the 4th Kingdom to replace the true Church of God, of which Jesus is the head, with a false church. It is important to note that the ten horns and the little horn both represent the 4th Kingdom, and it is the little horn that speaks, "great words against the highest and shall wear out the Saints of the highest and think to change times and laws." The little horn will change times by developing a theology that points away from the fulfilling of the prophecy through miseducating the people/populace. For example, he unleashes the worst persecution against the Saints that the world has ever seen or will see while at the same time teaching the populace that the "great persecution, that the Saints of the highest endured and is still in the midst of when they stand against the false church and its false theology is still to come sometime in the future. He changed laws by superimposing his own culture and laws upon the entire world. His theology teaches that a world government will be established sometime in the future, when in fact, the world government is already in place. He used art to Europeanize Jesus, the Messiah. All his painting, sculptures, and other religious art represents Europeans. Greek and Roman gods replaced the early prominent Saints such as Peter, Paul, James, and John. Daniel, chapter eight, verse eleven through thirteen tells us that this evil ruler "magnified himself even to the prince of host, and by him the daily sacrifice was taken away, and the place of his sanctuary (God) was cast down, and a host was given him against the daily sacrifice by reason of transgression and cast down the truth to the ground; and practiced and prospered." There are four concepts one must define and identify in the aforementioned verses; "The daily sacrifice, truth, transgression, and the place of his sanctuary."

The "daily sacrifice," refers to the replacing of the true Church of God which is in Jesus with a false church that leads people to hell/destruction under the leadership of Satan, the dragon. Hebrews chapter 4, verses 14-16, establishes the priesthood of Jesus the Messiah. "Seeing then that we have a great high priest, that is past into the heavens, Jesus the Son of God, let us hold fast our profession. For we have not a priest which cannot be touched with feelings of our own infirmities; but was in all points tempted like as we are, yet without sin. Let us therefore, come boldly unto the throne of grace, that we may obtain mercy, and find grace to help in time of need." Here is a picture of Jesus, who offered his own blood and body as our own daily sacrifice, so that He might become our high priest forever after the order of the Melchizedek. Hebrew chapter 5, verse. 7-10, says: "Who in the days of his flesh, when he had offered up prayers and supplications with strong crying and tears unto him that was able to save him from death and was heard in that he feared. Though he were a son yet learned obedience by the things which He suffered; and being made perfect, (complete) He became the author (high priest) of eternal Salvation unto all of them that obey him; Called of God a high priest after the order of Melchizedek.

Hebrews chapter seven gives a good description of Melchizedek in verses one through three: "For this Melchizedek, King of Salem, priest of the most high God, who met Abraham returning from the slaughter of the King, and blessed him; first being by interpretation King of righteousness, and after that also King of Salem, which is, King of peace; without father, without mother, without descent, having neither beginning of days, nor end of life but, made like unto the son of God; abideth a priest continually. In summary regarding Melchizedek, he is without father, without mother, without descent, having neither beginning of days, nor end of life; but made like unto the Son of God who is a priest continually (forever). The first chapter of the Gospel of St. John tells us who Jesus really is in verses 1-4. "In the beginning was the word, and the word was with God, and the word was God. The same was in the beginning with God. All things were made by him; and without him was not anything made that was made. In him was life; and the life was the light of men."

The above verses show that Jesus, the only begotten Son of God, possesses all the attributes of Melchizedek, the high priest. Jesus is the

Word of God, meaning He is without mother, without father (earthly father), without descent, having neither beginning of days, nor end of life. Verses 12-14 of St. John chapter one says: "But as many as received him, to them gave He power to become sons of God, even to them that believe on His name: which were born, not of blood, nor of the will of the flesh, nor of the will of man, but of God. And the word was made flesh and dwelt among us…full of grace and truth." Verse thirteen here is extremely important. Looking at each of these phrases one clearly sees that "born, not of blood," means Jesus did not come from Joseph's sperm, nor Mary's egg, which would have been of blood. Jesus had to be without sin in order to qualify as our continuing high priest. Joseph's sperm and Mary's egg both carried the original seed of sin passed down from Adam. "Nor the will of the flesh," means that Joseph and Mary did not commit fornication to bring about Mary's conception. "Nor the will of man," shows that Mary was not unfaithful to Joseph, nor was she raped. "But of God," demonstrates the majesty of our Heavenly Father when He takes the fertilized seed prepared from the foundation of the world and implanted it into Mary's womb so that Jesus could experience everything that man goes through from conception, (fertilized egg attached itself to the wall of the woman's womb) to death. Hence, Mary became a surrogate mother for Jesus. In St. Luke chapter one, verse thirty-five, the Angel tells Mary: "The Holy Ghost shall come upon thee, and the power of the highest shall overshadow thee: therefore, also that holy thing which shall be born of thee shall be called the Son of God." Just as God did with Adam when he put him into a deep sleep before taking one of his ribs with which Eve was made (Genesis 2:21-22), so he overshadowed Mary after the Holy Ghost had come upon her and implanted the seed (word) in her womb. Notice three persons were involved in this surgery, the Holy Ghost, the power of the highest, and the Word which was to become a quickening spirit (life- giving spirit) in the flesh. The Word would take on the "likeness of sinful flesh" in order to condemn sin in the flesh. He did not take on sinful flesh, but only the likeness of sinful flesh, in Him was no sin at all." (I Corinthians 15:45, I Peter 3:18; Ephesians 2:1-5, Colossians 2:13; John 5:21; 6:63). Hence, Jesus indeed possesses all the characteristics attributed to Melchizedek. He was without mother, without father, without descent, neither was there beginning of days, nor end of life because he was made a quickening (life-giving) spirit. As high priest, Jesus is the only one who received the Holy Spirit in the fulness without measure (John 3:34, 35). Hence, the taking away of the "daily sacrifice," refers to replacing of the true Church of God which is in Jesus with the false church that leads man to destruction. "Casting the truth down to the ground," means that the beast and those who follow him do not obey Jesus' commands. Jesus is the truth, therefore, by refusing to obey Him means that you have abandoned God's truth. This happened when the false church Europeanized Jesus and replaced his first apostles with pictures and sculptures of the Roman and Greek gods. The transgression is called, "the transgression of desolation," in Daniel chapter eight (8) and verse thirteen (13), it is also called the "abomination of desolation" and the "abomination that maketh desolate," in Daniel chapter eleven (11) in verse thirty-one and again in chapter twelve, verse eleven. Jesus calls it the "abomination of desolation," in Mark 13:14 and Matthew 2:4-15. The sanctuary refers to the Holy of Holies or the presence of God. So, the place of His (God's) sanctuary being cast down means the way into God's presence has been blocked or taken away by the teachings of false theology, which when people follow, they cannot enter into the presence of God. Hence, the place of the sanctuary is in the hearts of men, i.e., the church in you. By making war with the Saints of the highest and overcoming them (the great persecution), and afterward replacing the Church of Jesus with a false church and a false doctrine/theology, the beast has blocked the only way into the Holy of Holies or God's presence.

Look at Daniel 8:23-25, we find three characteristics of the fourth beast/ world power that must be explained: "not in his own power, cause crafts/trade to prosper, and with a false peace shall destroy many." First, the beast/world power does not rule in his own power. The question is: in whose power does he rule? To answer this question, we must look at the 13th chapter of Revelation. Revelation 13:1-2 says: "I saw a beast rise up out of the sea, having seven heads and ten horns, and upon his horns ten crowns, and upon his head the name of blasphemy…And the dragon gave him his power and his seat, and great authority." This is the same description of the fourth beast in Daniel, Chapter 7. When Daniel informs us that this beast/world power does not rule in his own power, the Apostle John adds more detail telling us that the beast gets his power from the dragon/Satan. Satan gave the beast his power, his seat, and great authority. The 4th beast/world power will cause crafts/trade to prosper. This corresponds to Babylon, the great in Revelation 18:1-3. Notice that the beast causes crafts to prosper all over the world except those nations who refuse to worship his name, image, or receive his mark in their foreheads or in their hand (we will discuss this later). Notice, Chapter 18, verses 11-13, all the merchandise that is being traded globally. The last part of verse 13 is extremely important. The beast will not only trade in material items, but in immaterial things as well. He trades horses, chariots, slaves, and souls of men. Men become slaves within this world system which controls everything, through religion, economics, education, and politics. All men become paid slaves working for the system implemented by the world system. Any nation who refuses to accept the world system will get squeezed out. (We will discuss this later). This system makes merchandise out of the "souls of men." According to Daniel 8:25, this fourth world power shall destroy many nations with a false peace. In other words, this world power offers peace through a false religion while also destroying peoples and cultures and taking lands and resources.

Therefore, Daniel says the 4th beast/world power is diverse (different) from all the world powers that was before it. Those world powers that preceded the 4th world power primarily used their military might to destroy and conquer other nations, but the 4th beast/world power becomes a superpower by merchandising men and the souls of people through a false religion, miseducation, economics, and politics. Jesus refers to this world power/era (4th beast) as "this generation", (Matthew 23:36; 24:34). Throughout the rest of this book, we will use the terms "this generation" and "the last generation"synonymously to refer to the present era which is the last opportunity for mankind to be reunited with the heavenly Father. This is the era of the preaching of the everlasting gospel of Jesus, the Messiah. God's plan of Salvation for mankind may be divided into two epochs, Pre-Christ, and Post-Christ. Pre-Christ refers to the godly believers who believed in God and his promises of a coming Messiah who would reunite all mankind who believe in him, with the heavenly father: believe that he is the Son of God, born of a virgin, and that the heavenly Father raised him from the dead. These are the Saints of the Pre-Christ/Pre-Messiah era. These are the ones to whom Jesus, the Messiah, preached and let out of captivity, (Satan's bondage in hell), and took back with him after his resurrection. These are identified in Matthew 27:50-53; "...and the graves were opened; and many bodies of the Saints which slept arose, and came out of the graves after his resurrection, and went into the holy city and appeared unto many. These represent the Saints from old Israel, from the 12 tribes." Revelation, Chapter 7, verses 1-8 reads: "...and I heard to the number of them that were sealed: an hundred and forty and four thousand of all the tribes of the children of Israel..." This one hundred forty-four thousand are the Saints of the Pre-Messianic age. They are the Saints who rose from the dead after Jesus' resurrection. Bear in mind that Jesus, the Messiah was present in both the Pre-Christian era and the Post-Christian era, but he was manifested in the "likeness of sinful flesh," only in the Post-Christian era. He visited/ came to earth on two occasions in the Old Testament. He met Abraham as Melchizedek and entered the fiery furnace to rescue the three Hebrews Hananiah, Mishael, and Azariah. Revelation, Chapter 7, verses 9, 13, and reads: After this I beheld, and lo, a great multitude, which no man could number, of all nations, kindreds, people, and tongues stood before the throne, and before the lamb, clothed with white robes with palms in their hands…and one of the elders answered, saying, unto me, "What are these which are arrayed in white robes? And whence came they?" and he said unto me, "These are they which came out of great tribulation, and have washed their robes, and made them white in the blood of the lamb."

This great multitude which no man could number, who came out of the great tribulation and have washed their robes in the blood of the lamb, represent the Saints of the Post-Christian era. This is also the era of the preaching of the everlasting Gospel of Jesus, the Messiah, which is the present or last generation. These are those who trust and obey Jesus, the Messiah, and believe that Jesus is the Son of God, and that the Father raised him from the dead. This is the new Israel which includes all mankind. They become Abraham's seed by faith in Jesus, the Messiah, who is the seed of Abraham. Hence, we become children of Abraham by faith in Jesus, the Messiah, and by obeying his commandments. The Jews and the Gentiles are made one by faith in Jesus, the Christ. This is what Jesus meant when he told the Jews of His time: "other sheep I have which are not of the fold: them also I must bring, and they shall hear my voice and there shall be one-fold and one Shepherd." Now, let us talk about the church in generation Post-Christ. Revelation, chapter twelve gives us a clear picture of the church in both the Pre-Christ and Post-Christ eras. However, we will concentrate on the church/Saints in the Post- Christ generation. Chapter 12, in the Book of Revelation gives a very succinct, compact view of the dragons attempt to take everything that belongs to

God, the Heavenly Father so that he can be like the Heavenly Father/ God. The woman in verse one and two, (chapter 12) represents old Israel, the earthly descendants of Abraham to whom the Heavenly Father/God made the promise of Salvation for all mankind, when He promised him that through his seed (Jesus), all the earth would be blessed. Abraham's importance in God's plan of Salvation for mankind is underscored in three important events that occurred in Abraham's life. First, God allowed Sarah and Abraham to give birth to Isaac when they were well past child-bearing age. Abraham was one hundred years old, and Sarah was ninety years old when he was born. Secondly, God would not destroy Sodom and Gomorrah without first telling Abraham. Genesis 18: 17-18 reads: "and the Lord said, shall we hide from Abraham that thing which I do; seeing that Abraham shall surely become a great and mighty nation (new Israel) and all the nations of the earth shall be blessed in him?"

Thirdly, Jesus in the form of Melchizedek introduced himself to Abraham as he returned from the slaughter of the kings. Although Jesus, the Lamb of God, had not been manifested in the likeness of sinful flesh, he is already active in God's plan of Salvation for mankind. Revelation 13:8 calls him "the lamb slain from the foundation of the world." Old Israel was pregnant with Jesus (the seed) from the time God made the everlasting covenant with Abraham until he was brought forth in the likeness of sinful flesh. So, from God's promise to Abraham to Jesus' birth by Mary, the church is travailing in faith and pained to be delivered. Verses three and four identifies "a great red dragon, having seven heads, and ten horns, and seven crowns upon his heads. This is the same beast in Daniel that represented the fourth earthly Kingdom and the last one before the coming of the "ancient of days." Verse 4 reads: "And his tail drew a third part of the stars of heaven and did cast them unto the earth: and the dragon stood before the woman, which was ready to be delivered, for to devour her child as soon as it was born." Satan tried to destroy Jesus as soon as he was born. Herod murdered all the children in Bethlehem, two years and under trying to kill Jesus. However, Joseph had been forewarned by an Angel of God to "flee into Egypt," to avoid Herod's genocide, (St. Matthew 2:13-18). Revelation chapter twelve verse five and six says: "And she brought forth a man child, who was to rule all nations with a rod of iron: and her child was caught up unto God, and to his throne. And the woman fled into the wilderness, where she had a place prepared of God…" Here, Jesus not only survived in a hostile world, but he finished His work on earth which His Heavenly Father assigned Him, and afterward ascended to God and to His throne. It seems that the "great red dragon" wanted to prevent the Salvation of mankind by keeping Jesus, the Lamb of God from offering himself as the ransom for mankind. Satan started his attack on mankind in Eden when he entered the serpent and deceived Eve, even calling God a liar. Having failed in his master plan to prevent the paying of ransom for mankind, Satan started an all or nothing war in heaven against the Angels, and, of God. Verses 7-9 says: "And there was war in heaven: Michael and his Angels fought against the dragon; and the dragon fought, and his angels, and prevailed not; neither was their place found anymore in heaven. And the great dragon was cast out… which deceiveth that whole world: he was cast out into the earth, and his angels were cast out with him." Hence, Satan leads an insurrection in heaven against the heavenly Father. The "great dragon," was created by God to minister (as well as all the angels of God), "to them who shall be heirs of salvation," Hebrews 1:7, 14. Notice that this heavenly war did not take place until after Jesus came in the likeness of a sinful flesh and "for sin, condemned sin in the flesh." The "great red dragon" was not defeated until after Jesus had shed his blood and offered his body as an offering/ransom (Hebrews 10:5, 10). So, Jesus, the Messiah, paid the ransom for everything in heaven and earth when he offered up himself once for all. Thus, after His resurrection, Jesus could claim all power in heaven and earth. Even in heaven according to Revelation 12:11, Michael and his angels overcame the "great red dragon" by the blood of the Lamb, and by the word of their testimony. Before discussing the church on earth after Jesus' ascension back to the Father, we will look at just who this "great red dragon" really is. What was his ministerial role in heaven before his insurrection against the heavenly Father, and what was his heavenly name and why was he cast out of heaven? Looking at Ezekiel, Chapter 28, verses 2-19; we can get a very clear description of the Cherub who became the dragon, and Satan, and the devil. Verses 2-5 reads: "Son of man, say unto the prince of Tyre, thus saith the Lord God; 'Because thine heart is lifted up, and thou hast said, I am God, I sit in the seat of God, in the midst of the seas: yet thou art a man, and not God, though thou set thine heart as the heart of God." Here is a being called the Prince of Tyre, whose heart is lifted up to the point that he thinks of himself more highly than he ought to. He lays claim to God's person and God's seat. God's response is that "Though you set your heart as the heart of God; you are just a man." In a later verse we will see that this created being is not an earthly man, but in God's hands he is a man; he was created to serve/minister, not to be God. Verses 3 through 5 reads: "behold, thou are wiser than Daniel; there is no secret that they can hide from thee: with thy wisdom and with thy understanding thou hast gotten thee riches…gold and silver into thy treasures by thy wisdom and thy traffic…, and thine heart is lifted up because of thy riches." This created being (cherub) is wiser than Daniel, and men (mankind) does not have the ability to hide anything from him. With his great wisdom and understanding he has become very wealthy with gold and silver and other riches. "By thy great wisdom and traffic, thou increased thy riches." Traffic here means merchandising. But the question remains, In what was he merchandising? He already has gold and silver, and other riches. Jesus asked the question, " What will a man give in exchange for his soul," (Matthew 16:26). Jesus also asked another question in Matthew 16:26, "For what is a man profited, if he shall gain the whole world, and lose his own soul?" Apparently, a man's soul is worth more than the whole world. This trafficking refers to merchandising in the souls of men as will be shown later in the Book of Revelation. This trafficking of souls and gaining of riches (gold and silver, souls of men), started when the dragon, that old serpent called the devil, and Satan deceived Eve in the garden of Eden. Genesis 1:26-28 tells us that God gave Adam dominion (rulership) over the fish of the sea, over the fowl of the air, and over the cattle, and over all the earth, to replenish the earth and subdue it. Hence, we logically conclude that the serpent (dragon/Satan) deceived Eve who caused Adam to disobey God and eat the fruit from the forbidden tree, which resulted in the usurping of Adams' dominion/ authority by the serpent/dragon. So, instead of Adam being the Prince of the earth, the air, and the sea, the dragon/serpent/Satan becomes the Prince of the world (also called the Prince of the air). Hence, that source of his riches is the air, the earth, the sea, and the souls of men. The most precious or valuable of these being the souls of men. Now, let's look at verse 6 through 19 and see God's response to the serpent usurping of man's God-given authority and his insurrection against God, his creator. Verses 6-10 reads: "…thus saith the Lord God, because thou hast set thine heart as the heart of God; I will bring strangers upon thee, the terrible of the nations …wilt thou yet say before him that slayeth thee, I am God? But thou shall be a man, and no God, in the hand of him that slayeth thee. Thou shalt die the death of the uncircumcised …for I have spoken it," saith the Lord God. God tells the dragon/serpent because you caused man to sin against me, I will bring men upon you (man=strangers). Man was made a living soul while angels are spirits. Man, without communion with God is called uncircumcised and, thus, the serpent/dragon without communion with God will die uncircumcised without communion with the Father in heaven. God tells the dragon, just like man is weaker (a little lower than the angels), than you, you are also weaker than me (God). So, in God's hands the serpent is just like a man, and not a God. Men will draw swords, (the Word of God), "against thy wisdom, ...defile thy brightness." In other words, the serpent will have to work against God through the mortal bodies of mankind in the earth. He will not be allowed to use his angelic authority against mankind. He will have to possess the minds and bodies of mankind in order to carry out his deception in the earth. When Satan/dragon enters some child, woman, or man or even an animal, what one sees is not the beautiful covering cherub, but the essence of evil represented by the dragon who comes to steal, kill, and destroy. Hence, we see people possessed by the dragon/Satan doing strange things, i.e., bodies contorted and distorted in ways that are unhuman, such as turning the joints of the body in ways that are not normal, or crawling along the floor or ground with the human body moving like a serpent/snake. His beauty and brightness are defiled. He is only allowed to enter or possess mankind by first capturing his mind and thereby entering his heart and taking possession of his body, verses 12 and 13 reads: Son of man take up a lamentation upon the King of Tyre (dragon/Satan), ... thus sayeth the Lord God; Thou sealest up the sum, full of wisdom, perfect in beauty. Thou have been in Eden the garden of God; every precious stone was thy covering...the workmanship of thy tabrets and of thy pipes were prepared in thee in the day that thou was created. In these verses, we see how wise and beautiful Satan was in the beginning of creation. He is full of wisdom and complete/perfect beauty. He was in Eden, the garden of God, his clothing/covering was "every precious stone." His musical instruments, "tabret and pipes," were built into him when God, the Father created him. This created being, the cherub who became the dragon, was created "full of wisdom, complete in beauty, very wealthy (clothed with every precious stone, and gold), with the most perfect/complete organ ever created built into his person. Verses 14 and

15 reads: "Thou art the anointed cherub that covereth; and I have set thee so: thou wast upon the holy mountain of God; thou hast walked up and down in the midst of the stones of fire. Thou wast perfect in thy ways from the day that thou wast created, till iniquity was found in thee... The cherub/dragon/Satan was anointed by God, the Father to overshadow/cover the mercy seat of God. He was anointed to serve in the midst of the stones a fire (altar of God) upon the holy mountain of God. In Isaiah, Chapter 6, we get a glimpse into the purpose of the stones of fire when Isaiah realized his unpreparedness in the presence of the holiness of God. God had a special job for Isaiah to perform, but he first had to be cleaned from his sin/iniquity and anointed for his vocation/calling. How was this accomplished? When one of the seraphim took a live/fiery coal from the altar of God with tongs and touched Isaiah's lips with it, his iniquity was taken away, and his sin was purged. Notice here, that the seraphim had to use tongs to remove the live coal from the altar of God because he was not anointed to walk up and down in the coals/stones the fire. The dragon/Satan was created and anointed to serve there to do the job for which he was created. No doubt, the dragon in his anointing could have handled the live coal with his bare hands, because he was created for that purpose. Verses 16-19, give the reasons why the Heavenly Father/God, removed him from the holy mountain of God and the stones of fire. Merchandising led Satan to violence and sin, meaning he transgressed God, the Heavenly Father's command. God tells the dragon, "I will cast thee as profane out of the mountain of God: and I will destroy thee, O covering cherub, from the midst of the stones of fire." In other words, since the dragon/Satan refuses to acknowledge God's reverence, God will remove him from the mountain of God. His special anointing is taken away, and he is no longer allowed to walk or minister in the midst of the stones of fire. He is cast out of the mountain of God as profane (irreverent and worldly) and destroyed from the midst of the stones of fire. Verses 17-19 reads: "...I will

cast thee to the ground, I will lay thee before kings, that they may behold thee. Thou hast defiled thy sanctuaries by the multitude of thine iniquities, by the iniquity of thy traffic… I will bring thee to ashes upon the earth, in the sight of all them that behold thee. Thou shall be a terror, and never shalt thou be anymore." Because of the greatness of his sin and the hidden sin (iniquity) of his traffic, Satan/the great red dragon, is cast out of the heaven into the earth where he is allowed to terrorize those whose names are not written in the Lamb's Book of Life, until the ancient of days comes to retake his earthly kingdom and return it to his Christ and to the saints. In the end, Stan will be banished to the lake of fire forever and ever, and he shall be no more. This is when the lion shall eat grass like the lamb, and they shall lay down together. One last point to make before we look at Isaiah Chapter 14, is this, when Ezekiel says Satan is cast out from heaven because of the iniquity of his traffic, he is referring to the sin of merchandising in the souls of man as will be pointed out later in the book of Revelation. The great red dragon comes to steal, kill, and destroy the souls of man. Hence, the battle between God/good and the Devil/evil, is all about the souls of man. The angels were made spirits who are to "minister to them who shall be heirs of salvation." (Hebrews 1:7-14) So far in our study of the "great red dragon," we have shown how and why he was created, how and why he sinned against the Heavenly Father. We have shown him created for ministering in, "the midst of the stones of fire," upon the altar of God (holy mountain of God). We have demonstrated his presence in Eden, the garden of God where he deceived Eve thus making himself and all mankind the servant of sin under the dominion of Satan. So, the plan of salvation is God's plan to redeem man, who He created in His image, and after His likeness for His glory, so that man can once again be free, (St. John 8:32), to abide in the presence of God the Father and glorify Him in spirit and in truth. Furthermore, we have shown God's reaction/response to Satan's interference in man's communion/

relationship with God, the Holy Father. Satan, "the great red dragon," will be cast to the earth and ultimately be destroyed. Next, let us look at Isaiah 14:12-15. Verse 12 reads: "How art thou, fallen from heaven, O Lucifer, son of the morning! How art thou cut down to the ground, which didst weaken the nations!" In other words, "O Lucifer, son of the morning, (referring to his wisdom, brightness, and beauty discussed in Ezekiel Chapter 28), why did God the Father cast you out of heaven, out of the "midst of the stones of fire?" Why did God cast you into the earth? The answer is given in verses 13-14 which reads: "For thou hast said in thine heart, I will ascend into heaven, I will exalt my throne above the stars of God: I will sit also upon the mount of the congregation, in the sides of the north: I will ascend above the height of the clouds; I will be like the most High." The great red dragon said in his heart, I will rise in heaven, I will exalt my throne above the angels (stars) of God. He was not satisfied being an angel but wanted to reign over the other angels. I will sit upon the mount of the congregation in the sides of the north. His aim/goal is to occupy God's seat and throne above the heights of the clouds or the highest heaven where God sits. Being in heaven, in the very presence of God, and having witnessed his great glory, majesty, and holiness, the dragon/Satan couldn't imagine anything greater than God, the heavenly Father, so he states his ultimate goal, that is, "I will be like the most high." His intent was to usurp God's throne. God's response is still the same as shown in Ezekiel Chapter 28, "...thou shall be brought down to hell, to the sides of the pit (lake of fire, the second death)." In other words, Satan will be destroyed for his gross sin.

Now let's embark on a discussion of Revelation 12:12-17. Verse 12 reads: "...Woe to the inhibiters of the earth and of the sea! For the devil is come down unto you, having great wrath because he knoweth he hath but a short time." He is the great dragon, "that old serpent, called the devil, and Satan, which deceiveth the whole world," having been cast out of heaven, into the earth with his angels is very angry, and is aware that his time is short. Verse 13 tells us that: "...when the dragon saw that he was cast into the earth, he persecuted the woman which brought forth the man child, and to the woman were given two wings of great eagle, that she might fly into the wilderness into her place where she is nourished... from the face of the serpent." So, the serpent/dragon makes war against the church/saints (woman), but the Heavenly Father removes the church from the presence or authority of the dragon and provides for the church until he returns to redeem the earth. Jesus says it another way, "If ye were of the world, the world would love his own: but because you are not of the world, I have chosen you out of the world, therefore the world hateth you." In other words, the church/saints are in the world, but not of the world. The church is in the world, but not under the authority of the dragon. The church/saints are nourished by the comforter, "the Spirit of Truth, the Holy Ghost, whom the world cannot receive, because it seeth him not, neither knoweth him," St. John 15:16-17. In St. John 17:13-16, Jesus says, "... they are not of the world. Even as I am not of the world. I pray not that thou shouldest take them out of the world, but that thou shouldest keep them from the evil." So, the saints/church of God, in Jesus, is in the world to be witnesses of Jesus, the Messiah, that He is the only begotten Son of God, that He was lifted up from the earth when He laid down His earthly life as ransom for mankind; and that the Heavenly Father raised Him from the dead (He made Jesus a life-giving Spirit). Verses 15-16 says: "and the serpent cast out his mouth water as a flood after the woman, that he might cause her to be carried away of the flood... the earth helped the woman...and swallowed up the flood which the dragon cast out of his mouth." Here the serpent cast out of his mouth a multitude of false teachings/doctrines, to deceive the church/saints. The earth helped the church/saints opening her mouth swallowing the false teachings the dragon cast out of his mouth. The saints are in the earth, baptized with the Holy Ghost and fire to witness Jesus and counter all the dragons' false doctrines by allowing the world to see Jesus in the way they live their lives and behave in the world. The Spirit of Truth guides the saints into all truth. Thus, it is not possible for the very elect/saints to be deceived. So, in verse 17, we see that the dragon's response to the Holy Ghost's arrival on earth is to make war against the saints; those who obey the commandments of God, and witness Jesus the Christ in the earth.

Now, what is the nature of the war, which this very angry dragon makes against the saints? Revelation, Chapter 13 explains the nature of the war against the saints. In this discussion, we look at scriptures and history to describe the nature of the war against the saints as perpetrated by the dragon/Satan. We will demonstrate how the dragon gives power to the beast, which represent the last world/earthly power before the ancient of days/God comes to destroy all earthly powers and gives the rulership of the earth to the Son of Man/Jesus, who will rule forever and ever with His saints. We will describe how this fourth beast/world power morphs into a false church using all the sacred ordinances of the true church such as communion, baptism, and the new birth to cause the whole world to worship the dragon while they believe they are worshipping God, the Heavenly Father. We will explain what the number of the beast, 666, means; identify his image and identify his mark. In the book of Revelation, Chapter 13, we see the same beast that Daniel saw, representing the last earthly superpower that rules the world before Jesus' return. Verses 1-2 reads: "and I …saw a beast rise up out of the sea, having seven heads and ten horns, and upon his horns ten crowns, and upon his head the name blasphemy." This is the fourth world power who blasphemes heaven in the book of Daniel. Notice the seven heads/mountains blaspheme. Verse 2 reads: "…and the dragon gave him his power, and his seat, and great authority." Remember that the prophet Daniel has already informed us that, the fourth beast/world power would be diverse/

different from the three previous beasts/world powers, and he would not rule in his own power, (Daniel 8:24). Here in the book of Revelation, John identifies the source of this world power's authority. He receives his power, his seat, and his authority from the dragon/Satan. So far, we have two entities in the operation of the last world power before Christ's return: the dragon/Satan and the Holy Roman Empire representing the fourth earthly kingdom. These two, Satan and the Roman Empire represents the first and second six (6) in the number 666 of the beast. So, the first six (6) is Satan, while the second six (6) is the Roman Empire notice that the property of six is absolute, it does not change. It might look/appear different, but the power/property of the number six (6) is a six (6). Note that three plus three (3+3), four plus two (4+2), and five plus one (5+1), all look different, but they all equal the property of six (6). In other words, three plus three equals six, four plus two equals six, and five plus one also equals six. So, no matter how they appear, they are all equal to six. Verses 3-4 says: "and I saw one of his heads, as it were wounded to death; and his deadly would was healed, and all the world wondered after the beast. And they worshipped the dragon, which gave power unto the beast: and they worshipped the beast saying, "who is like unto the beast? Who is able to make war with him?" These two verses describe the problems the Roman Empire faced trying to survive as a world power. The city of Rome was overrun and ransacked by the Germanic tribes several times, but they made no attempt to occupy the city. This was not the deadly wound because the Germanic tribes were not in competition with Rome for world domination, rather, they fought in the Roman armies. Carthage in North Africa was in direct conflict with Rome for world supremacy. The Carthaginians military commander, Hannibal defeated the Roman army led by the Roman commander, Scipio, right up to the gates of Rome, but his government back in Carthage refused to send reinforcements, forcing Hannibal to return home before completing his conquest of Rome. While

Hannibal trained new elephants for war, Masinissa, his Nubian calvary leader sent intelligence to Scipio, Jr., telling him that if he attacked Carthage immediately before Hannibal finished training his war elephants, he could defeat Carthage. Scipio, Jr., sailed across the sea to north Africa before Hannibal's war elephants were ready and defeated the Carthaginian army. So, Rome took her place as the new world leader. This is the deadly wound from which the Roman Empire/the fourth beast recovered. Note, the ten horns representing ten kings (Germanic Tribes), were not wounded, but one of the seven heads received a deadly wound and was healed. This is the same beast/world power as the one in Revelation, Chapter 17:1-3, Daniel 7:7-8, and Revelation Chapter 13. In Revelation 17:1-6, there is a difference, the beast carries the woman full of names of blasphemy, dressed as royalty, i.e., "arrayed in purple and scarlet, decked with precious stones and pearls, and having a golden cup in her hand full of abomination and filthiness of her fornication." Revelation 17:9 reads: "…the seven heads are seven mountains, on which the woman sitteth." Revelation 17:18 says: "and the woman which thou sawest is that great city, which reignth over the kings of the earth." Using these two scriptural facts, we can identify the royal city that reigns over kings of the earth. The city of the beast/world power is identified as the city of Rome. Rome is famous for its location, straddling seven hills or mountains. There is no other royal/capital city of a world power that meets this description except Rome, Italy. Revelation 17:2 informs us that "the great whore" sits upon many waters," while Verse 15 tells us that the waters where the whore/woman sits are "peoples and multitudes, nations, and tongues." What is the relationship between the whore/woman and the peoples, multitudes, nations, and tongues? The answer is given in Revelation 17:2. It says, "…the kings of the earth have committed fornication with the whore/woman, "and the inhabitants of the earth have been made drunk with the wine of her fornication." Fornication in this context means we can only be married to one bride/church and that is the one of which Jesus, the Messiah, is the head. Allegiance or worship of God, to any other besides the Heavenly Father through His only begotten Son, Jesus, the Christ is "fornication." In Revelation 17:5-6, John, the Apostle of Jesus, reveals a name that is written on the woman's forehead, "Mystery, Babylon the Great, the mother of harlots and abominations of the earth. This is the mark of the beast/world power. Notice that it is written upon the forehead. The forehead is your mind. Those who follow the beast will receive a mark on their foreheads or in their hands. The hands represent one's actions. To capture your mind, the beast/world power has instituted a system of miseducation in order to control the people's minds and a system of intimidation and fear to cause people to act like he wants them to act. However, he (the beast/world power) tries to get rid of the true church of Jesus, the Christ, i.e., the early saints who are preaching and teaching the true gospel of Jesus, the Messiah. Hence, the great persecution of the saints has already begun and will continue until the ancient of days comes. The killing of early saints created a vacuum that was filled with a false church/religion that leads to destruction, and a theology that changes times and laws. Revelation 17:6 reads: "and I saw the woman (Rome) drunken with the blood of the saints, and with the blood of the martyrs of Jesus…" Thus, the beast. Holy Roman Empire, makes war against the saints of Jesus and overcomes them; not defeat them, because the true church cannot be defeated, (Jesus has already won the war.), but Jesus allowed the saints to be worn down and overcome for a "time of times, and the dividing of time," until the "Ancient of Days, God, comes and gives judgment to the saints. Constantine the Great was not the first or the only emperor who had a hand in the setting up of the state religion called Catholicism/Christianity. But Constantine the Great was the one who implemented the change from the Roman Empire to Catholicism/Christianity, the official religion of the Holy Roman Empire, thus, becoming the third 6 in the number of the beast (666). Revelation 17:8 says" "The beast that thou sawest was, and is not, and shall ascend out of the bottomless pit, and go into perdition: they that dwell on the earth shall wonder...when they behold the beast that was, and is not, and yet is." This verse describes how the beast/world power morphs from the Holy Roman Empire into the Catholic/Christian Church. The historians argued over the date for the fall of Rome or the western Roman Empire for a long time because no one could pinpoint a date as to when Rome fail. Finally, they agreed to set the date for the fall of Rome at A.D. 476, without any concrete proof for Rome's fall. I assert that there is no proof that Rome ever failed, simply, because Rome never failed! Therefore John calls the Roman Empire the beast that was, and is not, and yet is. The bottomless pit is Satan's seat where he will be imprisoned during Jesus' thousand-year reign on this earth. At the end of Revelation 17:8, John refers to the Holy Roman Empires as, "the beast that was, and is not, and yet is." What is the message that John is conveying to his readers? What John is pointing out here is, the Holy Roman Empire existed, recovered from a deadly wound (doesn't exist), but the deadly wound healed (should have died but didn't) and yet is (exist in another form that doesn't look like an empire). The western Roman Empire existed in the world for everyone to see; then it disappeared from everyone's sight; but it still exists in a different form with a different appearance. Now, we move back to Revelation Chapter 13, to further demonstrate how the western Holy Roman Empire morphed into a universal religion. In other words, the wolf is still a wolf, but now he is disguised in sheep's clothing. Revelation 13:4 says: "and they worshipped the dragon which gave power unto the beast: they worship the beast saying, who is like unto the beast? Who is able to make war with him?" Here we get a glimpse at the Roman Empire at its height after the defeat of Carthage, when all roads led to Rome; when she was expanding her empire into the western world, when no nation was able to make war with her. Chapter 13:5-6 reads: "and there was given unto him a mouth speaking great things and blasphemies…and he opened his mouth in blasphemy against God, to blaspheme His name, and His Tabernacle, and them that dwell in heaven." Remember, that we have identified the city of Rome, Italy, as the woman sitting on the beast with seven heads which are seven mountains upon which the city is founded. The Roman Empire was given power over the kingdoms of the world by Satan/the dragon in exchange for worship. Satan wants to be "like God." He wants man to worship him, like they worship God. This is his ultimate goal. When the dragon was cast into the earth from heaven, he was given authority over all men whose names are not written in the Lamb's Book of Life. Hence, the Roman Empire instituted "emperor worship," which means worship of the Roman Emperor and his gods. This is the worship of the beast. So, by worshipping the beast, you are also worshipping the dragon who is the source of his power. Satan attempted to foil God's plan of salvation for mankind by offering Jesus all the kingdoms of the world and the glory of them in exchange for worship. Jesus turned him down (Luke 4:5-8; Matthew 4:8-10). Revelation 13:7-8 reads: and it was given unto him to make war even with the Saints, and to overcome them: and power was given him overall kindreds, and tongues, and nations. And all that dwell upon the earth shall worship him, whose names are not written in the Book of Life of the Lamb slain from the foundation of the world." Beginning with the emperor Nero, the Roman Empire has been at war with the Saints of the Most High. The Roman Empire/the beast is allowed to overcome the Saints until God (The Ancient of Days) retakes his earthly Kingdom from the dragon/Satan and gives it to Jesus and his Saints. Here, to overcome the Saints does not mean that the beast/Roman Empire defeated the Saints. The Saints cannot be defeated by a foe who is already defeated. Jesus tells his Saints in John 16:33 to: "be of good cheer; I have overcome the world." So, to overcome the Saints, means that the Roman Empire is in charge of worldly affairs for a season and the Saints are in the world, but not of the world, therefore, the Saints are in the world which is under the dominion of the dragon/Satan and the beast/Roman Empire. So, as long as the Saints are under the earthly dominion of the beast/Rome Empire, they will be persecuted and have tribulation (John 16:33; I Timothy 3:12). The Saints of the Most High will be tried, persecuted, and have tribulation until the end of the present age. Hence, the Saints must exhibit much patience, while they are being tried in the fire/in the world. Those who endure to the end shall come forth as pure gold and inherit the earth with Jesus. Revelation 13:10 reads: "he that leadeth into captivity shall go into captivity. He that killeth with the sword, must be killed with the sword. Here is the patience and the faith of the Saints." John is not talking about physical captivity, but rather spiritual captivity. The sword used to kill people is not a physical sword, but the Word of God which gives life, because it is life. Jesus is the Word of God. When one leads people away from Jesus, the Christ, he is leading them into captivity. The Sword of the Spirit which is the Word of God is life and it gives life, but when misused or misapplied it leads to death. Paul admonishes us regarding Satan and his false apostles in II Corinthians 11:13-15, where he writes: "for such are false apostles, deceitful workers, transforming themselves into the apostles of Christ…for Satan himself is transformed into an angel of light. Therefore, it is no great thing if his ministers also be transformed as minister of righteousness…" Hence, we can conclude that Satan, the dragon, has an army of false apostles working to deceive mankind, and thus, steal, kill, and destroy the souls of men. Although, the dragon/Satan cannot of himself destroy a man's soul, yet he attacks the free will of a man by convincing him in his mind through miseducation to disobey God which is sin. Sin leads to death. The dragon/Satan has set up a false church on earth to mimic the true Church of Jesus and thereby lead men to hell and ultimately to the Lake of Fire which is the second death (the death of the soul). Jesus warns us in John 5:37 to, "search the scriptures; for in them ye think ye have eternal life: and they are they which testify of me." Again, Paul tells us in II Timothy 2:25, to "Study to show thyself approved unto God, a workman that needeth not to be ashamed, rightly dividing the Word of God." So, in Revelation 13:11-18, we show you how the dragon/Satan implemented his false church in the earth making full use of Jesus' name, and the sacred ordinances instituted by Jesus our Savior. Satan also implemented a system of theology, to accompany this false religion/church which leads men into captivity by controlling their minds and their free wills just as he did in Eden when he so boldly called God a liar and deceived Eve, and thus Adam, leading to the first death.

So far, we've identified and discussed the dragon as the first 6 in the trifecta (666). Now, we will look at Chapter 13 of Revelation in verses 11-18: Verse 11 reads: and I beheld another beast coming up out of the earth; and he had two horns like a lamb, and he spoke as a dragon." Jesus always spoke of His Saints/church as lambs and never associated them with any ravenous beast. Here we see a beast looking like a lamb with two lamb horns. The lamb horns here represent the authority of the false church, but not the Church of Jesus. This is a false church which was divided into East and West with the deadly purpose of controlling the minds of the whole world through its educational and theological systems which works together as one. This beast looking like a lamb is exposed as a wolf in sheep's clothing as soon as he opens his mouth and begins to speak. John informs us that when he speaks, he speaks as the dragon. This is further supported by Verse 12, which says of this second beast: "and he exerciseth all of the power of the first beast before him, and causeth all of them which dwell therein to worship the first beast..." The second beast is not a regular political entity in appearance, appears as the Church of

Jesus, and speaks as the dragon. Here is the third six, is clearly seen as the second beast gets his power from the first beast, who gets his authority from the dragon. Hence, we trace the locus of power as it moves from the dragon/Satan to the first beast/Roman Empire, and finally to the second beast/the false church with its false apostles who speaks as the dragon/Satan. So, we can conclude that this is the implementation of the church of Satan/dragon which imitates the Church of Jesus. This false Church represents the third six in the number 666, which is also the number of a man. Verses 13 and 14 says of the second beast: "And he doeth great wonders, so that he maketh fire come down from heaven on the earth in the sight of men, and deceiveth them that dwell on the earth by the means of those miracles which he had power to do in the sight of the beast; saying…, that they should make an image to the beast…"

Looking at this first in a historical context, we can remember Constantine the Great's vision of a flaming cross in the sky and an accompanying voice that said, "with this sign conquer." His soldiers also saw the phenomenon, hence, the miracle of the fire coming down from heaven in the sight of man. Note, that the source of the fire is the "great dragon/Satan. Dragons have the ability to exhale fire. This vision was also inspiration for making an image to the beast. Thus, we can conclude that the image of the beast is the cross symbol. The physical cross as an object of worship is blasphemy because the Saints worship the Father through His only begotten Son, Jesus. Saints do not worship the physical cross, nor an image of the physical cross. Saints preach that Jesus offered himself for the ransom of all mankind on the physical cross in order to fulfill the prophecy of the Old Testament. The physical cross is a symbol of death, not life. The significance of the physical cross is summoned up in John 12:32, which reads, in the words of Jesus: "and if I be lifted up from the earth, I will draw all men unto me." Jesus said this to signify how he would die. Jesus endured the physical cross, but He didn't bear it. The scripture tells us that Simon of

Cyrene carried the physical cross for Jesus. The physical cross bore Jesus, but the cross that Jesus bore was the things he suffered for us, including death on the cross. The image of the cross was used by the dragon/Satan to legitimize an illegitimate church on earth. Notice this vision of the flaming cross appeared after the Saints had been killed or decimated except for those who escaped to the mountains. Hence, Satan tried to replace the Church of Jesus with a false church that leads to death in the Lake of Fire. Note, that after the vision of the flaming cross, the cross symbol appears everywhere. It was atop every church. It was placed inside every church with a sculpture/image of a European Jesus on it. Everyone was forced to attend church when they heard the church bell toll. If they were caught not attending church, they were beaten, thrown in the dungeon, or even killed. Upon entering the church sanctuary, they were taught to fall on their knees and make a cross symbol across their bodies. Moreover, the soldier's swords were made in the shape of a cross; their breastplates and shields had crosses on them; their helmets were embellished with crosses; even the horses' bridles, saddles, and their saddle blankets were imprinted with crosses; all their clergy and representatives of the false church wore crosses around their necks and had crosses imprinted on their robes or other clothing. Hence, the cross symbol is identified as the image of the beast/Roman Empire/Catholic Church and is an object of worship. In Revelation, Chapter 13, verse 15, we are informed that the beast/Catholic Church had power to give life unto the image of the beast so that the image of the beast should both speak, and cause that as many as would not worship the image of the beast should be killed." The question here is, how does the beast give the image of the beast (the cross symbol) life and the ability to speak? A symbol is something that points beyond itself to something greater, i.e., the flag points beyond itself to a nation. The beast/Christianity uses pictures, paintings, sculptures, miseducation and theology to give the cross symbol/image of the beast life and the ability to speak. In other words, through miseducation and theology, the cross symbol is embedded in the minds of people. Those who believe in what they have been taught through miseducation and theology gives life and speaking ability to the cross symbol/image of the beast through their minds. What is in a person's mind and heart will be played out in their life through actions/life and speech. Constantine's toleration of all religions was the beginning of the implementation of a plan to use a false church to ensure the survival of the Western Roman Empire. Thus, after over two centuries of persecution, the true church is living in the caves and dens, and the mountains where Jesus told them to flee when they saw the abomination of desolation spoken of by the prophet Daniel. Thus, by the time of Constantine, a vacuum had been created by the declination of the true church. So, Constantine, as emperor begins to fill this vacuum with a false church by beginning a policy of toleration of all religions within the Roman Empire. Later, Constantine would use his power as emperor to persecute and kill those who refused to accept this false church. By the time of the emperor Theodosius I, this false church had become the official religion/church of the Holy Roman Empire. Christianity uses an army of monks, priests, nuns, and bishops to conquer bodies, minds, and souls of men. This is what John alludes to when he says in Revelation 13:9-10: "If any man have an ear, let him hear. He that leadeth into captivity shall go into captivity: He that killeth with the sword, must be killed with the sword. Here is the patience and faith of the saints." Here, John is not just referring to physical slavery, but also the capturing of minds and souls of men all over the world. Therefore, the Catholic Church/Christianity, placed such great emphasis on the evangelization/romanization of all non-Christians. The true church of Jesus has always been invisible, but the Catholic Church started by Constantine has always been visible with its focus of control centered in Rome with Christs' Saints decimated and scattered. Catholic/Christian church leaders taught that every Christian church had to agree with the church of Rome because Peter and Paul had founded the church of Rome. In fact, Peter was crucified in Rome, while Paul was beheaded there. Once the false church/Christian church had been fully implemented, leadership stratification appeared in the titles of deacon, priest, and bishop, and pope. Irenaeus, a church leader in Gaul declared that all churches should acknowledge the supremacy of the church of Rome. Remember, that previously Constantine had declared himself Bishop of the church of Rome. Once the supremacy of the church of Rome had been accepted or forced upon the Christians, the bishop of the church of Rome takes the title "Pope" which means papa, or father. Notice that the pope's crown or headdress has the image of the beast/the cross symbol on it. Irenaeus also tried to justify the supremacy of bishops using the concept of the "Apostolic succession." Irenaeus falsely claimed: that the apostles had appointed bishops as their successors, that these successors had in turn appointed their own successors.

When it comes to the church of Rome, Irenaeus claims that Peter and Paul appointed the first bishop of Rome. In the 5th Century, beginning with Leo I, the bishops of Rome began misusing the words of Jesus in Matthew 16:18-19, to support the concept of the Petrine doctrine; that Jesus made Peter the head of the catholic church and that Peter passed this power to the bishops of Rome. Thus, the Petrine doctrine gave further impetus to the idea of the supremacy of the church of Rome, eventually, leading to the full implementation of the concept that the church of Rome is supreme over all Christian churches, which led to the merging of all bishops in the Roman Catholic church with the "Pope" as the supreme ruler or king. This is the world system that is dominating world events today. This is the fourth beast or world power, which is different from other world powers spoken of by the prophet Daniel. This is the second beast from Revelation, chapter 13, who gets his power from the first beast/Rome Empire, who was given the power, the seat, and the authority of the dragon/Satan. This is the world system that traverses the entire globe, trading in material goods as well as in the bodies, minds, and souls of men. Ezekiel says that the beast/dragon became very wealthy through his much trafficking/trading, Revelation 13:16-17 reads: "And he causes all, both small and great, rich and poor, free and bond, to receive a mark in their right hand, or in their forehead: and that no man might buy or sell, save he that had the mark or the number of his name."

The primary question here is, what is the mark that the beast forces all people to receive in their right hands or in their foreheads? Most people are right-handed; so, the right hand represents one's actions. The forehead represents a person's mind, which is the gateway or the entrance to his heart. A person's mind and heart determine his actions. Thus, the beast/Christian/Catholic church controls the minds, hearts, and souls of people all over the world through its educational and theological teachings. Hence, the mark of the beast may be identified as the Christian education and theology. If a person has received the Christian schooling and believes in it, then the mark is in their forehead. However, a person educated in the Christian perspective, and does not believe in it, but acts as if he believes in it, has the mark of the beast in his right hand. In other words, he behaves like the system wants him to behave in order to get what he wants from the system. Therefore, this beast or world system controls the economics of the world through trade, and thereby forces the people to accept their theological and educational teaching or behave as if they do in order to participate in the world system of merchandising in material and immaterial goods. To reiterate, the mark of the beast is Christian theology and education. The name of the beast is Christianity. The number of his name is 666 which corresponds to the dragon/Satan, the Roman Empire, and the Catholic church. The locus of control rest with the dragon. The number 666 is also the number of a man. That man is Constantine the Great who implemented the transition from Roman

Empire to the Catholic or Christian empire. The Christian empire traversed the entire globe conquering, converting, and committing non-Christians into, "perpetual slavery," cognitively, spiritually, and physically by orders issued by the Roman Catholic church or the Christian empire. Note that the pope wielded power over the kings, and queens of the Christian empire. Thus, by issuing a series of papal bulls (official decree from the pope), the Roman Catholic Church used the "age of discovery" or the doctrine of discovery to change the destiny of countless of millions of people and confiscated their land and incorporated them into the worldwide Christian empire. In particular, two papal bulls (Roman Pontifex and Inter Cetera) issued by the catholic church gave orders to the Christian kings to conquer and convert indigenous people and/or place them into "perpetual slavery." Papal bull, "Roman Pontifex" was issued in 1452 by pope Nicholas V, to king Alfonso V of Portugal. The bull ordered King Alfonso V to declare war on all non-Christians throughout the world. Pope Nicholas V sanctioned and prompted the conquest, colonization and exploration, of non-Christian nations and their territories. Pope Nicholas V, also issued papal bull Dun Diverses which says: "We grant you (kings of Spain and Portugal) by these present documents, with apostolic authority, full and free permissions to invade, search out, capture and subjugate the Saracens and pagans and any other unbelievers and enemies of Christ wherever they may be, as well as, their kingdoms, churches, countries, principalities, and other property and to reduce their persons into perpetual servitude. (The Pope's Decree)

In 1493, Pope Alexander VI, issued papal bull Eximiae Devotion id giving Spain the same right and privileges relative to "discovery" as had been given to the Portuguese. Spain was to take possession of the lands in the west while, Portugal was to take possession of the lands in the east. Therefore, after studying the papal bulls, we deduce this truth; that the Catholic Church is nothing more than the Roman Empire disguised as the Church of God in Jesus, the Christ. Hence, the fourth beast of Daniel and the second beast is the Catholic/Christian Church. Daniel says it was diverse or different from all empires preceding it, while John tells us that it appears as Christ's Lamb but speaks as or for the dragon/Satan. The pity is that all the people who worship the beast are on their way to hell and to the Lake of Fire and they are not aware of it. It is different from all the great empires that preceded it because it uses religion as a front while it leads the body, mind, and soul into captivity. John informs us that this Christian empire known as Babylon the great or mystery Babylon trades all over the globe in material goods as well as, "slaves, and souls of men." (Revelation 18:11-13) John tells us again that after God (The Ancient of Days) has destroyed this Christian empire; "in her was found the blood of the prophets, and of the saints, and of all that were slain upon the earth." (Revelation 18:24) The fact that the blood of everyone who had been slain in the earth was found in her, denotes that the focus of authority was the dragon/Satan who is responsible for all deaths in the earth. He only comes, "to steal, kill, and destroy. (St. John 10:10)

In conclusion, Dal through the Holy Ghost has received answers to all his questions regarding Christianity, the Bible, the taking away of the daily sacrifice, the trodding down of the sanctuary, the last generation, the beast, the image of the beast, and the mark of the beast. Dal now understands the importance of understanding the answers to all these questions in order to ensure one's name is written the Lamb's Book of Life from the foundation of the earth. Dal has always said, "Follow me as I follow Jesus in the Holy Ghost." The one piece of advice Dal leaves with all readers of this book is: Be baptized in the Holy Ghost and then follow him into all truth. Expect persecution and tribulation in this world; but endure until Jesus comes/until the end, and you will be delivered/'saved. Jesus did not start a new religion; He brought salvation to all men who believe that He is the Son of God, and that God raised Him from the dead.

CPSIA information can be obtained
at www.ICGtesting.com
Printed in the USA
BVHW041350090522
636554BV00006B/41